Cloud Computing Fundamentals: Build and Deploy Apps in the Cloud

A Step-by-Step Guide to Understanding Cloud Platforms and Services

MIGUEL FARMER

RAFAEL SANDERS

Table of Content

TABLE OF CONTENTS

INTRODUCTION

Cloud Computing Fundamentals: Build and Deploy Apps in the Cloud

In recent years, cloud computing has become the cornerstone of modern technology, offering unparalleled flexibility, scalability, and efficiency to businesses of all sizes. As organizations increasingly rely on cloud infrastructure to power their applications, the need for a comprehensive understanding of cloud platforms, services, and architecture has never been more critical. This book, **"Cloud Computing Fundamentals: Build and Deploy Apps in the Cloud"**, is designed to provide a thorough exploration of the cloud computing landscape, empowering developers, IT professionals, and business leaders to harness the full potential of the cloud.

Why Cloud Computing?

Cloud computing has revolutionized the way organizations deploy and manage applications. By offering resources such as computing power, storage, and databases over the internet, cloud computing eliminates the need for on-premises hardware and infrastructure. This shift allows businesses to focus on innovation and core business functions rather than the complexities of managing physical servers and hardware.

The cloud's rise to prominence has enabled faster deployment cycles, global accessibility, and cost savings— key advantages in an increasingly digital world. Whether for building scalable web applications, hosting data storage, or providing high-availability services, the cloud has become an indispensable part of the modern tech ecosystem.

As businesses continue to migrate to the cloud, the demand for cloud-savvy professionals is on the rise. Understanding how cloud platforms work, the tools and services they provide, and how to integrate them into real-world applications is crucial to staying competitive in today's fast-paced tech landscape. This book aims to demystify cloud computing and provide practical, hands-on knowledge for building and deploying cloud-based applications.

Who Is This Book For?

This book is intended for a wide range of readers, including:

- **Aspiring Developers and Engineers**: If you are new to cloud computing and looking to build your first cloud application, this book will introduce you to the core concepts, tools, and technologies needed to get started.

- **Experienced Professionals**: For those with some cloud experience, this book offers deep insights into advanced topics such as serverless architecture, cloud orchestration, and disaster recovery strategies.
- **Business Leaders and Decision-Makers**: Understanding cloud computing is no longer just a technical skill—it's also a business imperative. This book provides insights into how cloud computing can drive business transformation, optimize costs, and improve operational efficiency.

Whether you are building a small-scale project, migrating a legacy application to the cloud, or designing enterprise-level solutions, this book will help you navigate the cloud landscape and leverage its capabilities to the fullest.

What You Will Learn

This book is organized into 27 chapters, each designed to take you step by step through the cloud computing journey—from foundational concepts to real-world applications. Key topics covered include:

- **Cloud Computing Fundamentals**: We begin by exploring the basic concepts of cloud computing, including the different service models (IaaS, PaaS, SaaS) and deployment models (public, private, hybrid). You will gain an understanding of how cloud computing works and how it's transforming industries across the globe.

- **Cloud Architecture and Design**: You'll learn how to design cloud applications that scale with demand. This includes understanding cloud infrastructure, networking, and storage, as well as how to architect applications for high availability and resilience.

- **Cloud Security**: As businesses move critical workloads to the cloud, security becomes a top priority. This book covers key cloud security principles, such as identity management, data encryption, and compliance, to help ensure your cloud applications are secure and compliant.

- **DevOps and Automation**: The book delves into how cloud services integrate with **DevOps** practices, focusing on automation for continuous integration and continuous deployment (CI/CD). You'll learn how to set up automated pipelines and integrate cloud services with tools like **Jenkins, Docker**, and **Kubernetes** to streamline application delivery.

- **Advanced Cloud Technologies**: In later chapters, we explore cutting-edge technologies such as **edge computing, quantum computing**, and **multi-cloud strategies**. You will see how these emerging trends are shaping the future of cloud computing and how they can be integrated into your cloud applications.

- **Real-World Case Studies**: The book includes real-world case studies from leading companies such as **Netflix** and **Airbnb**, showing how they leverage cloud technologies to scale their services, improve operational efficiency, and innovate in their respective industries.

- **Practical Examples**: Throughout the book, we provide practical, hands-on examples, including how to set up cloud services like **AWS S3, Google Kubernetes Engine**, and **Azure DevOps**. These examples allow you to see cloud technologies in action and guide you through setting up your own cloud-based applications.

Why This Book Matters

Cloud computing is not just a buzzword—it is a foundational technology that powers modern digital services, from the apps we use daily to the infrastructure that drives industries like healthcare, finance, and entertainment. As businesses continue to embrace the cloud, the ability to design, deploy, and manage cloud applications will become increasingly valuable.

However, understanding cloud computing requires more than just theoretical knowledge—it requires practical experience with the tools and technologies that power the cloud. This book fills that gap by providing you with a deep understanding of cloud concepts, practical examples, and the skills needed to build real-world applications that leverage cloud services.

A Roadmap for Success

Each chapter of this book is crafted to build upon the previous one, taking you on a journey through the fundamental concepts of cloud computing, the various tools and platforms available, and the advanced techniques for managing and deploying cloud applications. By the end of this book, you will not only understand the principles of cloud computing but also have the hands-on experience needed to confidently build and deploy cloud-based applications.

Who Should Read This Book?

This book is ideal for:

- **Developers** looking to move from traditional software development to cloud-native application development.
- **System Administrators** and **DevOps Engineers** interested in mastering the tools and strategies for automating infrastructure management in the cloud.
- **Business Leaders**, **Entrepreneurs**, and **IT Managers** who need to understand cloud computing's impact on business and technology strategy.

Whether you're starting your cloud journey or looking to deepen your expertise, this book is a comprehensive guide to mastering cloud computing.

Conclusion

The cloud is not just a trend; it's a revolution that is reshaping the way we think about technology and business. As cloud computing continues to evolve, staying ahead of the curve is essential for organizations and individuals alike. **"Cloud Computing Fundamentals: Build and Deploy Apps in the Cloud"** provides you with the tools, knowledge, and practical experience needed to succeed in this dynamic and rapidly changing field. By the end of this book, you'll be equipped to take full advantage of the cloud's potential and build applications that are scalable, secure, and future-proof.

Welcome to the future of computing. Let's dive in!

CHAPTER 1

INTRODUCTION TO CLOUD COMPUTING

Overview of Cloud Computing and Its Evolution

Cloud computing is the delivery of computing services over the internet, allowing businesses and individuals to access resources like servers, storage, databases, networking, software, and more, without the need to own or maintain the physical hardware. Instead of purchasing and managing their own data centers and servers, users can rent or lease access to computing resources hosted by cloud providers.

The evolution of cloud computing began in the 1960s, with the concept of shared computing resources. The idea was further developed in the 1990s with the rise of the internet and virtual machines. Early cloud services were focused on providing remote storage and email. However, with the improvement of internet speeds, virtualization technologies, and global infrastructure, cloud computing quickly expanded into the vast platform we know today.

In the early 2000s, companies like Amazon Web Services (AWS), Microsoft, and Google began offering public cloud services, making it easier for developers to deploy applications and manage resources in the cloud. Over the years, cloud computing has continued to evolve with the introduction of new models, such as serverless computing and artificial intelligence (AI) services, making it an essential part of the global IT landscape.

Benefits of Cloud Computing in Today's World

Cloud computing offers several significant benefits that have revolutionized how businesses and individuals operate:

1. **Cost Efficiency**: Cloud computing eliminates the need for businesses to invest in expensive hardware and IT infrastructure. Instead, they pay for cloud services on a subscription or usage-based model, making it more affordable for companies to scale their operations.

2. **Scalability**: Cloud services can quickly scale up or down based on demand. This flexibility ensures that businesses can handle spikes in traffic or growth without having to worry about capacity planning or expensive infrastructure upgrades.

3. **Accessibility**: With cloud computing, data and applications are accessible from anywhere with an internet connection. This improves remote work capabilities and allows users to collaborate in real-time.

4. **Security**: Many cloud providers invest heavily in security, offering features such as encryption, firewalls,

and identity management tools. These providers often adhere to strict security standards and offer better protection than many businesses could achieve on their own.

5. **Reliability**: Cloud providers typically offer high uptime guarantees and built-in disaster recovery options. With multiple data centers in different regions, cloud services can provide greater reliability than on-premises infrastructure.

6. **Innovation**: Cloud computing enables businesses to quickly adopt new technologies, such as machine learning, artificial intelligence, and big data analytics, without significant upfront investments. This accelerates innovation and helps businesses stay competitive.

Types of Clouds (Public, Private, Hybrid)

Cloud computing can be categorized into three main types, each offering different levels of control, security, and deployment options:

1. **Public Cloud**:
   o In a public cloud, the cloud infrastructure is owned and operated by a third-party cloud provider, such as Amazon Web Services (AWS), Microsoft Azure, or Google Cloud. These providers make resources like servers, storage,

21

and databases available to the public over the internet. Public clouds are cost-effective, as they follow a pay-as-you-go model, and are widely used by businesses of all sizes.

- o **Real-World Example**: A startup might use AWS to host its website and store data because of the low cost and scalability it offers. The company only pays for the resources it uses, scaling up or down as needed.

2. **Private Cloud**:

- o A private cloud is used exclusively by one organization. It can be hosted on-premises in the company's own data center or by a third-party provider, but it offers greater control and customization. Private clouds are often used by businesses that have strict security or compliance requirements, such as financial institutions or healthcare providers.

- o **Real-World Example**: A healthcare organization might use a private cloud to store sensitive patient data, ensuring that it meets privacy regulations and provides high levels of security.

3. **Hybrid Cloud**:

- o A hybrid cloud is a combination of public and private clouds, allowing data and applications to be shared between them. This approach provides businesses with greater flexibility and optimization by choosing the most appropriate cloud environment for each workload. For instance, sensitive data can be stored in a private cloud, while less critical workloads are run in the public cloud.

○ **Real-World Example**: A large enterprise might use a hybrid cloud to run most of its operations in the public cloud while keeping its financial records and customer data on a private cloud to ensure security and compliance.

Real-World Examples: How Companies Use Cloud Services

Cloud computing is used by companies across industries to improve efficiency, reduce costs, and innovate. Here are a few real-world examples:

1. **Netflix**:
   ○ Netflix, a leading streaming platform, uses AWS for its cloud infrastructure. With millions of users streaming content worldwide, Netflix relies on AWS's scalability and reliability to handle large amounts of data and video streams. The company uses AWS services for video transcoding, storage, and content delivery.

2. **Dropbox**:

   o Dropbox, a popular file-sharing and collaboration platform, uses cloud computing to offer users cloud storage and file synchronization. Users can access their files from anywhere, on any device, with Dropbox handling all the backend infrastructure in the cloud.

3. **Airbnb**:

   o Airbnb, the online vacation rental marketplace, uses cloud computing to manage its platform, process payments, and handle massive amounts of data about listings and users. By using cloud services, Airbnb can scale its platform quickly as the number of users and listings grows.

4. **Spotify**:

   o Spotify uses cloud computing to stream music to millions of users around the globe. The company uses cloud storage for its vast music library and utilizes cloud computing for data analytics to provide personalized recommendations to users.

Conclusion

In this chapter, we've introduced the fundamentals of cloud computing, its evolution, the benefits it provides, and the different types of clouds available to businesses. As we move forward in this book, we will dive deeper into how cloud computing is applied in real-world scenarios, providing step-by-step instructions on how to leverage cloud platforms and services to build and deploy applications.

CHAPTER 2

UNDERSTANDING CLOUD SERVICE MODELS

Cloud computing is not just about renting storage or hosting websites—it's about a wide range of services that can meet different needs and requirements. The three primary models of cloud computing—Infrastructure as a Service (IaaS), Platform as a Service (PaaS), and Software as a Service (SaaS)—offer different levels of abstraction, control, and responsibility for managing cloud resources. In this chapter, we'll dive into each model, explore their differences, and discuss when and why to use each one.

Explanation of Cloud Service Models

1. **Infrastructure as a Service (IaaS)**:
    o   **What it is**: IaaS is the most fundamental cloud service model, providing the basic building blocks of computing—servers, storage, networking, and other virtualized resources. With IaaS, you rent the infrastructure and have full control over the operating systems, applications, and middleware you install and manage. It's

similar to renting a physical server, but with more flexibility and scalability.

- **Key Features**: Virtual machines, storage, networking, load balancers, and firewalls. Users have control over the operating system, storage, and deployed applications.
- **Use Case**: IaaS is ideal for businesses that want to build applications from the ground up, need highly flexible environments, or have specific requirements for control over the infrastructure.

2. **Platform as a Service (PaaS)**:
- **What it is**: PaaS is a higher-level cloud service that abstracts away much of the infrastructure management. It provides everything you need to develop, test, deploy, and maintain applications, but without having to manage the underlying hardware or operating system. PaaS includes frameworks, databases, middleware, and development tools that help speed up the development process.
- **Key Features**: Application hosting, databases, development tools, application lifecycle management, and environment scaling. Users only manage the application code, while the platform handles the rest.

27

o **Use Case**: PaaS is great for developers who want to focus on building apps without worrying about infrastructure, operating systems, or scalability issues. It's typically used for developing web apps, mobile apps, and microservices.

3. **Software as a Service (SaaS)**:

o **What it is**: SaaS is the most complete cloud service model. It delivers fully managed applications to end users over the internet. With SaaS, you don't have to worry about infrastructure, platforms, or updates; everything is handled by the service provider. The application is ready to use out-of-the-box, and users simply log in and start working.

o **Key Features**: Ready-to-use applications, automatic updates, no infrastructure management, and multi-tenant environments (multiple users share the same instance of the application).

o **Use Case**: SaaS is ideal for businesses or individuals who need software solutions without dealing with any underlying infrastructure or complex setup. Examples include email services, customer relationship management (CRM) software, and collaboration tools.

Differences and Use Cases for Each Model

Service Model	Level of Control	Target Users	Key Use Cases	Examples
IaaS	High	IT professionals, Developers	Virtual machines, infrastructure management, scalable storage	AWS EC2, Microsoft Azure, Google Compute Engine
PaaS	Medium	Developers	Application development, deployment, microservices, web apps	Google App Engine, AWS Elastic Beanstalk, Microsoft Azure App Service
SaaS	Low	End users	Ready-to-use software applications, collaboration tools, CRM, email services	Google Workspace, Microsoft 365, Salesforce, Zoom

- **IaaS** gives users complete control over infrastructure, ideal for businesses with custom infrastructure needs or those looking to migrate their existing systems to the cloud.

- **PaaS** is designed for developers who need an environment to build and deploy applications quickly, with minimal concern for the underlying infrastructure.
- **SaaS** is for end-users who need software solutions without the hassle of installation, maintenance, or infrastructure management.

Example: Using AWS EC2 (IaaS) vs. Google App Engine (PaaS)

Let's take a look at how two popular cloud services from Amazon and Google differ when it comes to IaaS and PaaS.

AWS EC2 (IaaS)

- **What it is**: Amazon Elastic Compute Cloud (EC2) is an IaaS offering from AWS. EC2 allows users to rent virtual machines (called instances) in the cloud to run applications, store data, and host services. With EC2, users have full control over the operating system, security, and configuration.
- **How it works**: As an IaaS solution, EC2 gives you virtualized computing power, so you can launch instances of various sizes and configure them as needed. You have

to manage the operating system, patching, and scaling of resources yourself.

- **Example Use Case**: A startup building a custom web application needs a highly flexible environment where they can control the operating system and software stack. They use EC2 instances to host their app, and they manually scale up resources during high traffic periods.

Google App Engine (PaaS)

- **What it is**: Google App Engine (GAE) is a PaaS offering from Google. It allows developers to deploy and manage web applications and services without worrying about the underlying infrastructure. GAE abstracts away the infrastructure management and focuses on the application itself.

- **How it works**: Developers simply write their application code and upload it to Google's platform, and App Engine handles the rest—scaling the application, balancing the load, and even automatically applying patches.

- **Example Use Case**: A development team building a scalable web application without wanting to manage servers can use Google App Engine. They can deploy the app, and App Engine will handle scaling the application based on user demand automatically.

Key Differences:

- **Control**: With AWS EC2, you have complete control over the virtual machines and can configure them as you see fit, while Google App Engine abstracts away the infrastructure management and automates most of the processes.
- **Flexibility**: EC2 offers more flexibility because you can configure the operating system, install custom software, and fully control the environment. App Engine, on the other hand, is more opinionated and restricts you to using certain technologies that it supports.
- **Ease of Use**: Google App Engine simplifies deployment and management, making it ideal for developers who want to focus on code, not infrastructure. EC2 requires more management and setup, which can be a good thing for projects that require customization.

When to Use Each Model

- **IaaS** (e.g., AWS EC2) is best when you need full control over your infrastructure and want the flexibility to customize your environment. It's suitable for companies with specific infrastructure needs, like legacy app migrations, complex web applications, or data-intensive workloads.

- **PaaS** (e.g., Google App Engine) is perfect when you want to focus solely on developing and deploying your app without worrying about managing the underlying infrastructure. It's ideal for modern web and mobile applications, especially when scalability is key, and you want to leverage cloud-native tools.

Conclusion

In this chapter, we explored the three primary cloud service models: IaaS, PaaS, and SaaS. Each model offers distinct advantages depending on your needs, whether it's control over infrastructure, ease of development, or ready-to-use software solutions. Understanding these models is essential for choosing the right cloud services for your applications and business needs. In the following chapters, we will dive deeper into each model with practical examples and guide you on how to use them effectively for building and deploying applications in the cloud.

CHAPTER 3

KEY CLOUD COMPUTING CONCEPTS

Cloud computing is built on a set of foundational concepts that make it a flexible, efficient, and cost-effective solution for businesses and developers. In this chapter, we will explore four key concepts: **Virtualization**, **Multi-tenancy**, **Elasticity**, and **Scalability**. Understanding these concepts is essential for fully grasping how cloud environments function and how they provide their many benefits.

Virtualization

What   it   is:
Virtualization is the process of creating virtual instances of resources—like servers, storage, and networks—that would otherwise be physical. By using virtualization software (such as VMware or Hyper-V), a single physical machine can host multiple virtual machines (VMs), each running its own operating system and applications independently. This makes it possible to run multiple systems on a single hardware resource.

How   it   works:
A hypervisor sits between the hardware and the virtual machines.

It abstracts the underlying physical resources and allocates them to the virtual environments. This allows the resources of a single machine to be divided into many virtual machines, each acting as a separate system. For example, a single physical server might be used to run several virtual machines, each hosting a different application or operating system.

Benefits of Virtualization:

1. **Resource Optimization**: Virtualization maximizes the use of physical hardware, allowing organizations to run more workloads on fewer physical machines.

2. **Isolation**: Each virtual machine is isolated, so problems in one VM (like a crash or security breach) do not affect others.

3. **Flexibility**: Virtualization allows businesses to easily deploy new VMs, move them between physical machines, and allocate resources dynamically.

Example:

A business running a series of customer-facing applications might use virtualization to deploy multiple VMs on a single server, each VM hosting a different application (such as a database, web server, and API service). This setup reduces hardware costs and makes it easier to manage resources.

Multi-tenancy

What **it** **is**:
Multi-tenancy is a cloud architecture principle where a single instance of a software application serves multiple customers (tenants). Each tenant's data and configuration are kept isolated, but they share the same underlying infrastructure. This model is common in SaaS applications, where a single version of the application is hosted for many different users.

How **it** **works**:
In a multi-tenant environment, all tenants share the same cloud resources—computing power, storage, etc.—but their data is segregated logically. For instance, in a multi-tenant CRM platform, each customer (tenant) has access to their own data, but the underlying infrastructure, database servers, and application logic are shared.

Benefits of Multi-tenancy:

1. **Cost Efficiency**: Since multiple tenants share the same infrastructure, service providers can offer lower costs to each user.
2. **Easier Maintenance and Upgrades**: Updating the software for all tenants can be done at once, reducing the complexity and cost of maintaining separate instances for each tenant.

3. **Scalability**: Multi-tenancy allows cloud services to scale by simply adding more tenants to the shared environment without significant changes to the infrastructure.

Example:

Salesforce, a popular CRM platform, is a SaaS solution that operates in a multi-tenant architecture. Each business using Salesforce has access to their own data and configuration, but the platform itself runs on a shared infrastructure managed by Salesforce.

Elasticity

What   **it**   **is**:
Elasticity refers to the ability of cloud systems to automatically scale resources up or down based on demand. This characteristic is crucial for handling varying workloads without manual intervention. Elasticity ensures that cloud resources can be dynamically allocated or deallocated as needed to maintain optimal performance.

How   **it**   **works**:
Cloud platforms use auto-scaling to increase or decrease resources based on predefined metrics (e.g., CPU usage, memory consumption, or incoming traffic). For example, if a website

hosted in the cloud experiences a spike in traffic, the cloud platform automatically provisions additional instances to handle the load. When the traffic subsides, the extra resources are deallocated, reducing costs.

Benefits of Elasticity:

1. **Cost Optimization**: Resources are allocated only when necessary, ensuring that businesses only pay for what they use.

2. **Performance**: Elasticity ensures that applications remain responsive and perform well even during traffic spikes or fluctuations.

3. **Agility**: Businesses can quickly adapt to changing demands without needing to predict or manually scale infrastructure.

Example:

An e-commerce website hosted on AWS might experience a sudden surge in visitors during a sale. With elasticity, AWS can automatically spin up additional EC2 instances to handle the increased load. After the sale ends and traffic decreases, those additional instances are terminated, reducing costs.

Scalability

What **it** **is**: Scalability refers to the ability of a system to grow and manage increased demand without sacrificing performance or reliability. It involves adjusting the infrastructure to handle larger loads, which can be achieved either by adding more resources to a single machine (vertical scaling) or by adding more machines to the system (horizontal scaling).

How it works:

- **Vertical Scaling (Scaling Up)**: This involves adding more CPU power, RAM, or storage to an existing machine. For example, upgrading a server to a more powerful one.
- **Horizontal Scaling (Scaling Out)**: This involves adding more machines or instances to a network, distributing the load across multiple systems. For example, adding more EC2 instances to handle increased web traffic.

Benefits of Scalability:

1. **Improved Performance**: As workloads grow, scalable systems can add more resources to ensure continued optimal performance.

2. **Cost Efficiency**: Scalable systems allow businesses to start small and expand as needed, avoiding unnecessary upfront costs.

3. **Resilience**: Scalable systems can handle failures more gracefully by redistributing workloads among healthy instances.

Example:

A social media platform might start with a small set of servers to handle its users. As the platform grows in popularity, the system must be able to scale horizontally by adding more servers to distribute the load. This allows the platform to maintain performance even as the number of users increases.

How These Concepts Benefit Cloud Computing

Each of the key cloud computing concepts—**virtualization**, **multi-tenancy**, **elasticity**, and **scalability**—provides important benefits that make cloud computing attractive to businesses and developers:

1. **Resource Efficiency**: Virtualization and multi-tenancy allow cloud providers to efficiently manage hardware and resources. This increases resource utilization and reduces costs for end users.

2. **Flexibility**: Elasticity and scalability ensure that cloud systems can adapt to changing demands, whether it's increased traffic, larger datasets, or more users.

3. **Cost Control**: Cloud computing's ability to scale dynamically means that businesses only pay for the resources they need, avoiding costly overprovisioning and underutilization.

4. **Agility**: Cloud systems can scale up or down quickly, making it easier for businesses to respond to market changes, handle unexpected traffic spikes, or implement new features without worrying about infrastructure.

Example: Scaling Up/Down Resources Based on Demand

Let's consider an online learning platform during the start of a new semester. During peak registration times, the platform experiences a surge in traffic, with thousands of students accessing the site to sign up for courses. The platform's cloud infrastructure needs to scale up to accommodate the increased load, ensuring that students can register without delays.

Using **elasticity**, the platform's cloud service automatically scales up by launching additional virtual machines or containers, which handle the excess traffic. After the registration period ends and traffic returns to normal, the system **scales down** by terminating the extra resources, reducing costs.

This automated scaling process is managed by the cloud platform, so the business doesn't have to manually intervene to ensure that performance stays optimal during busy periods.

Conclusion

In this chapter, we explored some of the most important concepts behind cloud computing: **virtualization**, **multi-tenancy**, **elasticity**, and **scalability**. These principles are essential for creating efficient, flexible, and cost-effective cloud systems. As we continue with the book, we'll see how these concepts are applied in real-world cloud services and platforms to provide businesses with the tools they need to build, deploy, and manage applications in the cloud.

CHAPTER 4

CLOUD COMPUTING ARCHITECTURE

Cloud computing architecture is the foundation upon which all cloud services are built. It is a combination of physical and virtual components that work together to deliver cloud services to users. In this chapter, we will explore the key infrastructure components of cloud computing, including servers, storage, networking, and databases. We will also break down how cloud hosting providers set up data centers to ensure performance, reliability, and scalability.

Understanding Cloud Infrastructure Components

Cloud computing architecture is built upon various components that are distributed across multiple data centers. These components work together to provide the fundamental cloud services—whether it's hosting a website, storing data, or running applications. Below is an overview of the core infrastructure components that make up cloud computing.

1. Servers (Compute Resources)

- **What they are**: Servers in the cloud are virtualized computing resources that provide the processing power needed to run applications and services. Unlike traditional physical servers, cloud servers are virtual machines (VMs) or containers that run on physical hardware in data centers but are abstracted and managed by cloud providers.

- **How they work**: Cloud providers offer a variety of server types (instances) based on the needs of the users. These servers can be configured with different amounts of CPU, memory (RAM), and storage to meet the requirements of different workloads. Virtual machines (VMs) are the most common way to run servers in the cloud, but newer technologies like containers (using Docker or Kubernetes) offer lightweight, scalable alternatives.

- **Benefits**: Cloud servers provide on-demand scalability, flexibility, and cost-efficiency. Users only pay for the resources they use, and servers can be quickly spun up or down as needed.

2. Storage (Data Storage Solutions)

- **What it is**: Cloud storage allows data to be stored remotely on the cloud provider's infrastructure instead of on local physical devices. Cloud storage is highly scalable and can handle large amounts of data. It typically includes several types of storage, including object storage, block storage, and file storage.

- **How it works**: Cloud storage services use distributed systems to store and manage data across multiple locations. For instance, object storage like Amazon S3 (Simple Storage Service) stores data as objects, while block storage like Amazon EBS (Elastic Block Store) provides disk storage that can be attached to virtual machines.

- **Benefits**: Cloud storage is scalable, durable, and accessible from anywhere with an internet connection. It is often more cost-effective and reliable than traditional storage solutions because cloud providers offer built-in redundancy and backup systems.

3. Networking (Cloud Network Infrastructure)

- **What it is**: Networking in cloud computing refers to the connections between different components of the cloud, including virtual networks, servers, storage, and other resources. Cloud providers offer networking services that ensure seamless communication between virtual machines, storage, and users on the internet.

- **How it works**: Virtual networks are created within the cloud environment to connect resources securely. Cloud providers offer various networking services like Virtual

Private Cloud (VPC), load balancers, firewalls, and Content Delivery Networks (CDN) to optimize communication between services, provide security, and reduce latency.

- **Benefits**: Cloud networking enables high-performance, secure communication and reduces the need for expensive physical networking infrastructure. It is also highly flexible, allowing for rapid changes to network configurations without needing hardware changes.

4. Databases (Cloud Databases and Data Management)

- **What they are**: Databases in the cloud allow users to store and retrieve data efficiently. Cloud databases are typically either relational (SQL-based) or non-relational (NoSQL-based), and they are managed and maintained by the cloud provider.
- **How they work**: Cloud providers offer managed database services, such as Amazon RDS (Relational Database Service) or Google Cloud SQL, which handle tasks like backups, scaling, and software patching. NoSQL databases like Amazon DynamoDB or Google Firestore are designed to handle large, unstructured datasets that scale horizontally.
- **Benefits**: Cloud databases offer high availability, automatic backups, and elastic scaling, meaning they can grow and shrink with demand. They also provide

developers with powerful features like automated database management and real-time performance monitoring.

How Servers, Storage, Networking, and Databases Work in the Cloud

Cloud computing relies on an interconnected set of components that provide a wide range of services, from computing power to data storage and network security. Let's break down how each component interacts within the cloud environment:

- **Servers (Compute Resources)**: When a user wants to run an application or service, the cloud provider spins up virtual machines (VMs) or containers to handle the computing workload. These servers are dynamically provisioned based on the user's needs (e.g., for high traffic or during off-peak times). These virtual servers interact with cloud storage for data retrieval and management, and communicate with other services through the cloud network.

- **Storage**: Cloud storage acts as the backbone for data in the cloud. Data generated by applications, databases, or user interactions is stored across distributed storage systems. Cloud storage is elastic, meaning it can grow automatically as data storage needs increase. This storage is accessible to the computing resources and can be connected via virtual network services.

- **Networking**: Cloud networking ensures that all cloud resources, such as virtual machines, storage, and databases, can communicate with each other securely and efficiently. Virtual Private Clouds (VPCs) allow users to create isolated networks within the cloud where all resources can interact with each other privately. Load balancing and routing ensure that traffic is distributed efficiently across servers, while firewalls and security groups manage access to resources.

- **Databases**: Cloud databases provide a secure, scalable, and easily manageable way to store structured (SQL) and unstructured (NoSQL) data. These databases interact with cloud compute resources (virtual machines) to retrieve or store data for applications. For example, an e-commerce website might store customer data in a relational database (SQL) while using a NoSQL database for product catalogs or customer reviews.

Example: Breakdown of How Cloud Hosting Providers Set Up Data Centers

Cloud hosting providers like Amazon Web Services (AWS), Microsoft Azure, and Google Cloud rely on a network of data centers strategically located around the world. These data centers house the physical infrastructure (servers, storage devices, networking equipment) that powers cloud services. Here's a breakdown of how cloud hosting providers set up and manage their data centers:

1. Physical Infrastructure

- **Servers**: The data center is equipped with high-performance servers that can be virtualized to run multiple virtual machines (VMs) or containers.
- **Storage**: Multiple types of storage systems (object, block, file storage) are used to store large amounts of data, ensuring high availability and redundancy.
- **Networking Equipment**: Data centers are interconnected with high-speed networking equipment, including routers, switches, and firewalls. This ensures efficient communication between servers and seamless access to the internet for users.

2. Redundancy and Failover

- **Backup Power**: Data centers are equipped with redundant power supplies, including backup generators and uninterruptible power supplies (UPS) to ensure constant uptime.

- **Cooling Systems**: To prevent overheating, data centers use advanced cooling systems to maintain the optimal temperature for servers and networking equipment.

- **Geographical Redundancy**: Cloud providers set up multiple data centers across different geographical regions, with each center having failover mechanisms in place. If one data center goes down, the system automatically shifts workloads to another active data center, ensuring business continuity.

3. Scalability and Elasticity

- Cloud hosting providers have designed their data centers to allow easy scaling. Servers, storage devices, and networking components are modular, allowing providers to add or remove resources as needed to meet customer demand.

4. Security

- Data centers are protected with physical security measures, such as surveillance cameras, security guards, and biometric access control systems. In addition, cloud providers implement advanced network security protocols (e.g., encryption, firewalls, DDoS protection) to safeguard data and communication within the cloud.

Conclusion

Cloud computing architecture is composed of various components, including servers, storage, networking, and databases. These elements work together in a dynamic and interconnected system that allows businesses and developers to leverage powerful cloud resources. The cloud infrastructure is designed to be flexible, scalable, and reliable, offering a range of services that help users build, deploy, and manage applications without worrying about the underlying hardware. In the next chapters, we will explore how to utilize these resources effectively to deploy and scale applications in the cloud.

CHAPTER 5

POPULAR CLOUD PROVIDERS

Cloud computing has grown exponentially, with several major players dominating the market. The leading cloud providers—**Amazon Web Services (AWS)**, **Microsoft Azure**, and **Google Cloud Platform (GCP)**—offer powerful and flexible services for businesses of all sizes. Each platform has its unique strengths, pricing models, and features. In this chapter, we will explore the major cloud providers, highlighting their key features, differentiators, and how they compare in terms of pricing and services.

Overview of Major Cloud Platforms

1. Amazon Web Services (AWS)

What **it** **is**: Amazon Web Services (AWS) is the largest and most widely used cloud computing platform in the world. It was launched by Amazon in 2006 and has since expanded into a vast array of services, ranging from compute and storage to machine learning, IoT, and AI. AWS has data centers spread across multiple regions, offering customers high availability and global coverage.

Key Services:

52

- **EC2 (Elastic Compute Cloud)**: Scalable virtual servers that allow users to run applications in the cloud.

- **S3 (Simple Storage Service)**: Object storage with virtually unlimited scalability, ideal for storing data, backups, and media files.

- **RDS (Relational Database Service)**: Managed SQL databases, including support for MySQL, PostgreSQL, SQL Server, and Oracle.

- **Lambda**: A serverless compute service that runs code in response to events without provisioning or managing servers.

- **IAM (Identity and Access Management)**: A service that allows users to securely control access to AWS resources.

Strengths:

- **Extensive Service Offering**: AWS offers a broad range of services, making it suitable for almost any type of business or use case.

- **Global Reach**: AWS has the largest number of data centers across various regions and availability zones, providing a highly redundant and reliable infrastructure.

- **Market Leadership**: As the first major cloud provider, AWS has an extensive track record and ecosystem with a large community of users and developers.

2. Microsoft Azure

What   it   is: Microsoft Azure is the cloud platform developed by Microsoft, which offers a comprehensive suite of cloud services, including computing, storage, networking, databases, and developer tools. Azure is highly integrated with Microsoft's software products, such as Windows Server, SQL Server, and Office 365, making it a strong choice for businesses that are already using Microsoft technologies.

Key Services:

- **Azure Virtual Machines (VMs)**: Flexible and scalable virtual servers for running applications.
- **Azure Blob Storage**: A highly scalable object storage solution for storing large amounts of unstructured data, such as videos and backups.
- **Azure SQL Database**: A fully managed relational database service based on SQL Server.
- **Azure Functions**: A serverless compute service that runs code in response to events without managing infrastructure.
- **Azure Active Directory (AD)**: Identity and access management service used to authenticate and authorize users.

Strengths:

- **Hybrid Cloud Solutions**: Azure offers strong hybrid cloud capabilities, allowing businesses to combine on-premises data centers with cloud resources.
- **Enterprise Integration**: Azure is deeply integrated with Microsoft's enterprise software, making it a natural choice for businesses using Microsoft products like Windows Server, SharePoint, and Dynamics.
- **Enterprise-Ready**: Azure is particularly well-suited for large enterprises with complex IT infrastructures.

3. Google Cloud Platform (GCP)

What **it** **is**: Google Cloud Platform (GCP) is the cloud offering from Google, known for its strength in data analytics, machine learning, and artificial intelligence services. GCP is also recognized for its high-performance computing and storage services. It is often favored by startups, developers, and organizations that require powerful data processing and analytics tools.

Key Services:

- **Google Compute Engine (GCE)**: Scalable virtual machines for running applications and workloads.

55

- **Google Cloud Storage**: Object storage for storing and accessing data, with high durability and low-latency access.

- **BigQuery**: A fully managed data warehouse that allows for real-time analytics on massive datasets.

- **Google Kubernetes Engine (GKE)**: A managed service for deploying, managing, and scaling containerized applications with Kubernetes.

- **Google Cloud Functions**: A serverless compute service for executing code in response to events.

Strengths:

- **Data and AI Focus**: GCP is known for its data analytics, machine learning, and AI tools, making it ideal for data-driven applications.

- **Innovative Tools**: Google's cloud platform leverages the same technology that powers Google Search, Gmail, and YouTube, offering advanced tools for big data and analytics.

- **Cost Efficiency**: GCP is often seen as a more affordable option compared to AWS and Azure, especially for data-intensive workloads.

Key Features and Differentiators

Each cloud platform has its unique strengths, and the right choice depends on the specific needs of your business or project.

AWS:

- **Strengths**: Extensive service catalog, global infrastructure, strong enterprise adoption, and a vast ecosystem.
- **Best For**: Businesses requiring a wide range of services, startups, enterprises, and businesses with complex infrastructure needs.

Azure:

- **Strengths**: Integration with Microsoft products, strong hybrid cloud support, and enterprise readiness.
- **Best For**: Businesses already using Microsoft products and services, enterprises looking for hybrid cloud solutions, and organizations focused on security and compliance.

GCP:

- **Strengths**: Advanced data analytics, machine learning, and AI tools, cost-effective pricing for data processing, and strong Kubernetes support.

- **Best For**: Startups, developers, and data-driven businesses that need cutting-edge data processing, machine learning capabilities, and high-performance compute resources.

Example: Comparing Pricing Models and Services

Pricing models across cloud providers can vary significantly, depending on the resources and services being used. Let's compare how AWS, Azure, and GCP approach pricing for some core services like computing, storage, and databases.

1. Compute Pricing (Virtual Machines)

- **AWS EC2**: EC2 instances are billed based on the instance type, the region in which they run, and the time the instance is running. AWS offers On-Demand, Reserved, and Spot instances. Reserved instances can offer significant discounts for long-term usage.
- **Azure Virtual Machines**: Azure VMs are billed similarly, based on the instance type, region, and usage. Azure also offers Reserved Instances with discounts for longer commitments.
- **Google Compute Engine**: GCP offers flexible pricing with per-second billing and sustained-use discounts. GCP

also offers preemptible VMs (similar to AWS Spot Instances) for cost savings on non-critical workloads.

2. Storage Pricing

- **AWS S3**: Pricing is based on the storage amount, the number of requests (e.g., PUT, GET), and data transfer. S3 offers different storage classes (e.g., Standard, Glacier) to optimize costs.
- **Azure Blob Storage**: Similar to S3, Azure Blob Storage pricing is based on the amount of data stored, the frequency of access, and the type of storage used (e.g., Hot, Cool, Archive).
- **Google Cloud Storage**: GCP offers pricing based on storage type (Standard, Nearline, Coldline), with similar cost structures to AWS and Azure. GCP's pricing model can be more straightforward, and it offers automatic data lifecycle management to optimize storage costs.

3. Database Pricing

- **AWS RDS**: Pricing depends on the database engine (e.g., MySQL, PostgreSQL), the instance size, and the storage. AWS RDS also offers an option for Reserved Instances at a discount.

- **Azure SQL Database**: Azure's pricing is based on the performance tier (e.g., General Purpose, Business Critical), storage, and provisioned compute resources.
- **Google Cloud SQL**: GCP's pricing is based on instance type, storage, and usage. Like Azure, GCP offers flexible scaling options based on demand.

Example Comparison:

Suppose you need to deploy a web application with a simple database back-end. Let's say you need one virtual machine with 2 vCPUs, 8 GB of RAM, and 100 GB of storage. Here's how the pricing might compare across providers (note that prices may vary based on region and usage patterns):

- **AWS EC2**: The cost of an On-Demand EC2 instance with the specified configuration might be around $0.096 per hour. S3 storage for 100 GB of data could cost approximately $2.30 per month.
- **Azure VM**: A similar Azure VM instance might cost around $0.085 per hour. Azure Blob Storage for 100 GB could cost around $2.30 per month.
- **Google Compute Engine**: The same instance on GCP would cost around $0.070 per hour. Google Cloud Storage for 100 GB would cost about $2.40 per month.

Although the pricing is competitive, GCP often offers lower pricing for long-term sustained usage, while AWS provides the most extensive service portfolio, and Azure offers superior integration with Microsoft products.

Conclusion

In this chapter, we explored the major cloud providers—**AWS**, **Microsoft Azure**, and **Google Cloud Platform**—and compared their services, strengths, and pricing models. Each cloud platform offers unique advantages, so choosing the right one depends on your specific needs. AWS is a great all-around option with a vast array of services, Azure excels for hybrid and enterprise environments, and GCP stands out for data-driven applications and machine learning workloads. By understanding the key features and pricing models of each provider, you can make an informed decision that aligns with your business goals.

CHAPTER 6

SETTING UP YOUR FIRST CLOUD ENVIRONMENT

Getting started with cloud computing can feel daunting at first, but the process is relatively simple, and cloud providers offer user-friendly interfaces that make setting up an environment a smooth experience. In this chapter, we will walk through the steps to sign up for a cloud provider, set up an account, and navigate the platform. We will also guide you through deploying a simple static website as a real-world exercise to get hands-on experience with cloud services.

Steps to Sign Up for a Cloud Provider

Signing up for a cloud provider involves creating an account, selecting a payment method (if required), and choosing the appropriate plan based on your needs. Let's go through the steps for signing up for the three major cloud providers: **AWS**, **Azure**, and **Google Cloud Platform (GCP)**.

1. Amazon Web Services (AWS)

- **Step 1**: Go to the AWS homepage at aws.amazon.com and click on **"Create a Free Account"**.

- **Step 2**: Enter your email address, choose an account name, and set up a password.

- **Step 3**: Provide billing information (credit card) for verification. AWS offers a **Free Tier** that includes many services with limited usage, so you won't incur charges unless you exceed these limits.

- **Step 4**: Choose a support plan. You can start with the **Basic** plan, which is free.

- **Step 5**: Complete identity verification by receiving a phone call or text to input a verification code.

- **Step 6**: Once verified, you can log into the AWS Management Console.

2. Microsoft Azure

- **Step 1**: Visit the Azure homepage at <u>azure.microsoft.com</u> and click on **"Start Free"**.

- **Step 2**: Sign in with a Microsoft account or create a new one.

- **Step 3**: Provide billing details (credit card) to verify your identity. Azure also offers a **Free Account** with limited credits and free services for the first 30 days.

- **Step 4**: Complete the security check (e.g., phone number verification).

- **Step 5**: Once set up, you can access the Azure portal to manage your cloud resources.

3. Google Cloud Platform (GCP)

- **Step 1**: Visit the GCP homepage at cloud.google.com and click on **"Get Started for Free"**.
- **Step 2**: Sign in with your Google account or create a new one.
- **Step 3**: Provide billing information (credit card). Google Cloud offers **$300 in credits** for new users, which can be used for any services within the first 90 days.
- **Step 4**: Set up your project in the Google Cloud Console, and you are ready to begin using the platform.

Basic Setup of an Account and Navigating the Platform

Once you've signed up for your chosen cloud provider, the next step is to navigate the platform. All cloud providers have a web-based console where you can manage resources, services, and billing.

Navigating AWS Management Console

- After logging into your AWS account, you will be directed to the **AWS Management Console**. This is your dashboard for managing all AWS resources.

- The **"Services"** menu is where you can access different cloud services like EC2, S3, RDS, etc.

- Use the **Search bar** at the top to quickly find a specific service.

- You can monitor your usage, view billing information, and manage IAM roles (for security) directly from the console.

- The **CloudWatch** service helps you monitor your AWS resources and applications, providing you with detailed metrics.

Navigating Azure Portal

- After signing into your Azure account, you will be directed to the **Azure Portal**.

- The portal offers a **dashboard** that provides an overview of your resources, billing, and notifications.

- The **"Create a Resource"** button lets you deploy a variety of services, such as virtual machines, databases, or storage.

- Use the **Search bar** to find services, and the **Azure Marketplace** provides third-party applications that can be deployed directly into your environment.

- The **Azure Cost Management + Billing** section allows you to monitor your spending and usage.

Navigating Google Cloud Console

- Once you log in to GCP, you will land on the **Google Cloud Console**.

- The **Navigation menu** on the left allows you to access services like Compute Engine (for virtual machines), Cloud Storage, BigQuery, and more.

- The **Cloud Shell** provides a command-line interface for managing resources, and it's pre-configured with tools like `gcloud` for interacting with your environment.

- The **Billing** section provides insights into your resource consumption and available credits.

Real-World Exercise: Deploying a Simple Static Website

In this exercise, we will deploy a simple static website using cloud storage. This website can consist of basic HTML, CSS, and JavaScript files. We'll demonstrate the process on **AWS S3**, **Azure Blob Storage**, and **Google Cloud Storage**.

1. AWS – Deploying a Static Website on S3

- **Step 1**: Log into the **AWS Management Console** and go to the **S3** service.

- **Step 2**: Create a new **S3 bucket**. Give it a unique name (e.g., `my-static-website-bucket`).

- **Step 3**: In the bucket settings, go to the **Properties** tab and enable **Static website hosting**. Specify the index document (e.g., `index.html`).

- **Step 4**: Upload your website files (HTML, CSS, JS) into the S3 bucket.

- **Step 5**: Set the appropriate permissions for your bucket to make it publicly accessible (you'll need to update the **Bucket Policy**).

- **Step 6**: After uploading, you can access your website via the S3 endpoint provided in the **Static website hosting** section.

2. Azure – Deploying a Static Website on Blob Storage

- **Step 1**: Log into the **Azure Portal** and go to **Storage Accounts**.

- **Step 2**: Create a new **Storage Account** and select the **StorageV2** option. Ensure that **Blob storage** is selected during creation.

- **Step 3**: After the storage account is created, go to the **Blob service** section and enable **Static website hosting**.

- **Step 4**: Specify the index document (e.g., `index.html`) and the error document (optional).

- **Step 5**: Upload your website files to the **$web** container within your storage account.

- **Step 6**: You will get a public URL to access your static website hosted on Azure Blob Storage.

3. Google Cloud – Deploying a Static Website on Google Cloud Storage

- **Step 1**: Log into the **Google Cloud Console** and navigate to **Cloud Storage**.
- **Step 2**: Create a new **Bucket** for your static website. Make sure to choose a unique name.
- **Step 3**: After creating the bucket, click on **Edit website configuration** in the **Bucket Details** section.
- **Step 4**: Specify the **index.html** and **error.html** files for your static site.
- **Step 5**: Upload your website files (HTML, CSS, JS) to the bucket.
- **Step 6**: Set the appropriate **permissions** to make your website publicly accessible by configuring the **Bucket Policy**.
- **Step 7**: Use the public URL provided by Google Cloud Storage to view your static website.

Conclusion

In this chapter, we learned how to sign up for a cloud provider, set up an account, and navigate the platform's console. We then walked through deploying a simple static website on three popular cloud platforms—AWS, Azure, and Google Cloud—giving you hands-on experience with the cloud's basic services. Deploying a static website is just the beginning; cloud platforms offer countless possibilities for more complex applications, databases, and infrastructure management. As you continue to explore cloud computing, you'll unlock even more powerful features that can help you scale and manage your applications efficiently.

CHAPTER 7

CLOUD SECURITY ESSENTIALS

As cloud computing becomes increasingly popular, securing cloud environments is more critical than ever. The flexibility and scalability of the cloud offer immense benefits, but they also introduce potential security risks. In this chapter, we will cover essential cloud security concepts—such as **identity management**, **encryption**, and **firewalls**—and explore best practices for securing cloud infrastructure. Finally, we will walk through an example of implementing **role-based access control (RBAC)**, a critical security feature in cloud environments.

Key Security Concepts in the Cloud

1. Identity Management

What   it   is:
Identity management (IdM) in the cloud involves ensuring that only authorized users and systems can access cloud resources. It is the process of creating, managing, and deleting identities, as well as assigning the appropriate access levels to those identities. Effective identity management is key to ensuring the integrity and security of cloud applications and services.

How **it** **works**:
Cloud providers typically offer **Identity and Access Management (IAM)** services that help administrators define and manage users, groups, roles, and policies. IAM allows businesses to enforce **least privilege access**, meaning users are granted only the permissions necessary for their specific role or function.

Benefits:

- **Control Access**: IAM helps ensure that only authorized users can access cloud resources.
- **Granular Permissions**: With IAM, permissions can be assigned at various levels (e.g., read-only access, admin rights) and customized based on the user's role.
- **Security Auditing**: IAM provides detailed logs of access requests, which can be used for auditing and identifying potential security threats.

2. Encryption

What **it** **is**:
Encryption is the process of converting data into a coded format that can only be read or deciphered by authorized parties. In the cloud, data encryption is essential to ensure that sensitive data remains protected both in transit (while being transmitted) and at rest (when stored on cloud servers).

How   it   works:
Cloud providers offer **encryption-at-rest** and **encryption-in-transit** as part of their security features:

- **Encryption-at-Rest**: Encrypts data stored on cloud servers (e.g., files, databases). This ensures that even if data is accessed by unauthorized parties, it remains unreadable without the decryption key.
- **Encryption-in-Transit**: Protects data as it travels across networks (e.g., when users access cloud applications or transfer files). This is typically done using **Transport Layer Security (TLS)** or **Secure Sockets Layer (SSL)** protocols.

Benefits:

- **Data Protection**: Ensures sensitive data, such as personal or financial information, is secure from unauthorized access.
- **Compliance**: Many regulatory frameworks (e.g., GDPR, HIPAA) require the encryption of sensitive data to meet compliance standards.
- **Confidentiality and Integrity**: Encryption ensures that only the intended recipients can access or modify the data, preventing data breaches or tampering.

3. Firewalls

What   it   is:
A **firewall** is a network security system that monitors and controls incoming and outgoing network traffic based on predefined security rules. In the cloud, firewalls act as a barrier between a trusted internal network (your cloud resources) and untrusted external networks (e.g., the internet).

How   it   works:
Cloud providers offer both **network firewalls** and **application firewalls**:

- **Network Firewalls**: These protect the cloud network by filtering traffic based on IP addresses, ports, and protocols. They can restrict access to cloud resources from specific sources or geographic locations.
- **Application Firewalls**: These protect specific applications (e.g., web applications) by filtering traffic based on application-layer protocols and inspecting the content for security threats (e.g., SQL injection, cross-site scripting).

Benefits:

- **Access Control**: Firewalls control who can access your cloud resources and block unauthorized users.

73

- **Threat Detection**: Firewalls can detect and block malicious traffic, such as DDoS attacks or unauthorized access attempts.
- **Layered Security**: Firewalls add an extra layer of security by preventing unauthorized access at the network or application level.

Best Practices for Securing Cloud Infrastructure

To effectively secure cloud environments, it's essential to follow industry best practices that focus on protecting both cloud infrastructure and the data stored within it. Here are some key practices to consider:

1. Apply the Principle of Least Privilege

The principle of **least privilege** means giving users and systems the minimum permissions necessary to perform their tasks. This limits the potential for misuse or unauthorized access. Regularly review access controls to ensure that users only have access to the resources they need and remove any unnecessary permissions.

2. Use Multi-Factor Authentication (MFA)

Multi-factor authentication adds an extra layer of security by requiring users to provide two or more forms of verification when logging into cloud systems. These factors may include:

- Something the user knows (password).
- Something the user has (a phone or hardware token).
- Something the user is (fingerprint or facial recognition).

Enabling MFA significantly reduces the risk of unauthorized access due to compromised credentials.

3. Regularly Monitor and Audit Access Logs

Monitoring and auditing access logs is critical to detecting and responding to security incidents in a timely manner. Cloud providers offer tools like AWS CloudTrail, Azure Monitor, and Google Cloud Logging that allow you to track user activity, resource usage, and potential security threats. Set up alerts for abnormal behavior or unauthorized access attempts.

4. Automate Security Policies and Updates

Cloud security should be proactive, not reactive. Automating security processes, such as applying security patches, configuring firewalls, and updating access policies, ensures that your cloud infrastructure is always up to date. Many cloud platforms offer services that can automate security management tasks.

5. Encrypt Data in Transit and at Rest

As discussed earlier, encryption is a crucial aspect of cloud security. Always ensure that sensitive data is encrypted both in transit and at rest. Use strong encryption algorithms and manage your encryption keys securely.

6. Regularly Backup Critical Data

Regular backups are essential to prevent data loss in case of an attack, failure, or breach. Many cloud providers offer automatic backup services for data and applications, ensuring that you can restore systems to a previous state if needed.

Example: Implementing Role-Based Access Control (RBAC)

Role-Based Access Control (RBAC) is a widely used method for restricting system access to authorized users based on their roles within an organization. By defining roles and assigning permissions to those roles, RBAC ensures that users have only the necessary access to resources.

Here's an example of how to implement RBAC in AWS, Azure, and GCP.

AWS IAM – Implementing RBAC

1. **Create IAM Roles**: In the **IAM** (Identity and Access Management) section of the AWS Console, create different roles based on your organization's needs (e.g., **Admin, Developer, Read-Only**).

2. **Assign Policies**: Attach policies to each role that define what actions users can perform. For example, the **Admin** role may have full access to all AWS services, while the **Read-Only** role may only allow viewing resources without making changes.

3. **Assign Roles to Users**: Assign users to roles based on their responsibilities. A developer may be assigned to the **Developer** role, while an IT admin would be assigned to the **Admin** role.

4. **Review Access**: Regularly review and update roles and policies to ensure that users have the appropriate level of access.

Azure RBAC – Implementing RBAC

1. **Define Roles**: In the **Azure Portal**, define custom roles or use built-in roles such as **Owner, Contributor**, or

Reader to assign permissions to users based on their responsibilities.

2. **Assign Roles**: You can assign roles at the subscription, resource group, or resource level, depending on the scope of access needed.

3. **Monitor Access**: Use **Azure Activity Logs** and **Azure Security Center** to monitor role assignments and detect any unusual activity.

Google Cloud – Implementing RBAC

1. **Create IAM Roles**: In **Google Cloud Console**, use the **IAM & Admin** section to create custom roles or use predefined roles like **Editor**, **Viewer**, or **Owner**.

2. **Assign Roles**: Assign roles to users at the project, folder, or organization level.

3. **Audit and Review**: Use **Cloud Audit Logs** to track and review role assignments and actions taken by users.

Conclusion

In this chapter, we explored essential security concepts in the cloud, including identity management, encryption, and firewalls. We also discussed best practices for securing cloud infrastructure, such as applying the principle of least privilege, using multi-factor authentication, and automating security policies. Lastly, we provided a practical example of implementing **role-based access control (RBAC)** to manage user access and protect sensitive cloud resources. By following these security practices and leveraging the cloud's built-in tools, you can ensure that your cloud environment is secure, compliant, and resilient against threats.

CHAPTER 8

CLOUD STORAGE SOLUTIONS

Cloud storage is a fundamental aspect of cloud computing that allows businesses and individuals to store, access, and manage data remotely. Unlike traditional on-premises storage solutions, cloud storage offers scalability, flexibility, and cost-efficiency. In this chapter, we will dive into the different types of cloud storage—**object storage**, **file storage**, and **block storage**—and explore the differences between local and cloud storage. We will also walk through a practical example of setting up a cloud storage bucket using **AWS S3**.

Understanding Object Storage, File Storage, and Block Storage

1. Object Storage

What   it   is:
Object storage is a storage architecture that stores data as objects rather than files or blocks. Each object consists of the data itself, metadata (information about the data), and a unique identifier (ID) for easy retrieval. Object storage is designed to handle large volumes of unstructured data, such as images, videos, backups, and log files.

80

How **it** **works**:
In object storage, data is stored in a flat namespace with a unique key or identifier. The data is divided into discrete objects, and each object is stored with metadata that describes its content, permissions, and other relevant information. Unlike file or block storage, object storage does not rely on a hierarchical file system. Popular examples of object storage systems include **AWS S3**, **Google Cloud Storage**, and **Azure Blob Storage**.

Benefits:

- **Scalability**: Object storage can scale horizontally, allowing you to store virtually unlimited amounts of data without worrying about physical limitations.
- **Durability and Availability**: Object storage services often replicate data across multiple geographic locations, ensuring high availability and redundancy.
- **Cost-Efficiency**: Object storage is typically more cost-effective than other storage types, especially for unstructured data.

2. File Storage

What **it** **is**:
File storage is a cloud storage service where data is stored as files in a hierarchical directory structure. It resembles traditional on-premises file systems, allowing users to organize and manage data

using directories and file paths. File storage is ideal for applications that require access to shared files, such as content management systems, collaborative environments, and legacy applications that rely on traditional file system structures.

How it works: In file storage, data is stored in a file system format that users are familiar with. It enables the use of common file protocols like **NFS (Network File System)** and **SMB (Server Message Block)** for accessing and managing files across a network. File storage services allow multiple users to access and share files simultaneously, often with built-in versioning and synchronization.

Benefits:

- **Compatibility**: File storage solutions are compatible with existing applications that require access to shared files.
- **Easy Management**: Since file storage uses a familiar file system, it is easy to manage and organize data.
- **Collaboration**: File storage allows multiple users or systems to access and collaborate on the same files in real-time.

3. Block Storage

What it is: Block storage divides data into fixed-size blocks and stores each block separately. Each block has its own address, and the system treats each block as an individual unit of storage. Block storage is commonly used for structured data, such as databases or virtual machines, where low latency and high performance are critical.

How   it   works: Block storage provides raw storage volumes that can be attached to virtual machines (VMs) and used as primary storage for databases, operating systems, and applications. It operates at a lower level than file storage and can be used to support high-performance workloads. Popular examples of block storage services include **AWS EBS (Elastic Block Store), Google Persistent Disks**, and **Azure Managed Disks**.

Benefits:

- **Performance**: Block storage offers high-performance capabilities, making it ideal for applications with high I/O operations, such as databases and virtual machines.
- **Flexibility**: Block storage can be resized, partitioned, and formatted to meet the specific needs of an application.
- **Low Latency**: Block storage typically offers low latency, making it suitable for performance-sensitive workloads.

Differences Between Local and Cloud Storage

While both local and cloud storage serve the purpose of storing data, they differ in several ways, including accessibility, scalability, and management.

1. Accessibility

- **Local Storage**: Local storage is tied to physical hardware, such as hard drives or SSDs, that are directly connected to a computer or server. Data is only accessible from the device that has the storage hardware installed.
- **Cloud Storage**: Cloud storage is accessible from anywhere with an internet connection, allowing users to access data remotely via a web interface or APIs. Cloud providers offer services with high availability and global access.

2. Scalability

- **Local Storage**: Scaling local storage requires physical upgrades, such as adding more hard drives or replacing existing ones. Scaling is limited by the physical infrastructure of the device.
- **Cloud Storage**: Cloud storage can be scaled virtually without limitations, as providers offer scalable solutions that automatically adjust to your storage needs. You only pay for the amount of data you store.

3. Cost

- **Local Storage**: The initial cost of local storage may be lower, but it involves ongoing maintenance, hardware upgrades, and potential capacity issues.
- **Cloud Storage**: Cloud storage typically follows a pay-as-you-go pricing model, where you only pay for the storage and bandwidth you use. This makes it more cost-effective for businesses with fluctuating storage needs.

4. Security

- **Local Storage**: Local storage relies on physical security measures and manual backups. While it can be secure, it requires ongoing maintenance to prevent data loss due to hardware failure, theft, or natural disasters.
- **Cloud Storage**: Cloud providers offer built-in security features, such as data encryption, redundancy, and automated backups. Cloud storage is often more secure than local storage due to the advanced security protocols employed by providers.

5. Backup and Recovery

- **Local Storage**: Backing up data on local storage requires manual processes, such as ing data to external drives or setting up complex backup systems.

- **Cloud Storage**: Cloud providers offer automated backup and disaster recovery solutions, ensuring that data is replicated across multiple locations for redundancy and recovery in case of failure.

Example: Setting Up a Cloud Storage Bucket with AWS S3

AWS S3 (Simple Storage Service) is one of the most popular object storage services in the cloud. In this example, we will guide you through the process of creating a storage bucket and uploading files to AWS S3.

Step 1: Log into the AWS Management Console

1. Sign in to your **AWS Management Console** using your credentials.
2. In the search bar, type **S3** and select the **S3 service** from the list.

Step 2: Create a New S3 Bucket

1. Click on **Create Bucket** to start the process.
2. **Bucket Name**: Choose a unique name for your bucket (e.g., `my-first-website-bucket`).

3. **Region**: Select a region where you want your bucket to be located. It's best to choose a region that's geographically close to your users to reduce latency.

4. **Bucket Settings**: You can configure various settings, such as versioning, logging, and encryption. For now, you can leave these at their default settings.

5. Click **Create Bucket** to create the bucket.

Step 3: Upload Files to the S3 Bucket

1. After the bucket is created, click on the bucket name to open the bucket.

2. In the **Objects** tab, click on **Upload**.

3. Choose the files you want to upload (e.g., HTML, CSS, and image files for a static website).

4. Click **Next** and configure any additional settings, such as permissions.

5. Click **Upload** to upload your files to the S3 bucket.

Step 4: Set Permissions for Public Access

1. To make your website publicly accessible, you need to update the permissions of the objects in the bucket.

2. Click on the **Permissions** tab, then click **Bucket Policy**.

3. Add a policy that allows public access to the files. A simple policy might look like this:

```
json
```

```
{
    "Version": "2012-10-17",
    "Statement": [
        {
            "Sid": "PublicReadGetObject",
            "Effect": "Allow",
            "Principal": "*",
            "Action": "s3:GetObject",
            "Resource":   "arn:aws:s3:::my-
first-website-bucket/*"
        }
    ]
}
```

4. Click **Save Changes** to apply the policy.

Step 5: Access the Files

1. After uploading the files and setting permissions, you can access your files via the **Bucket URL** provided in the **Properties** tab.

2. For example, if you uploaded an index.html file, you can access it by visiting:

bash

```
http://my-first-website-bucket.s3-
website-us-east-
1.amazonaws.com/index.html
```

Conclusion

In this chapter, we explored the three main types of cloud storage: **object storage**, **file storage**, and **block storage**, each serving different use cases and offering unique benefits. We also discussed the differences between local and cloud storage, highlighting the advantages of cloud solutions, such as scalability, accessibility, and cost-efficiency. Finally, we walked through a real-world exercise of setting up a cloud storage bucket with **AWS S3** to demonstrate how easy it is to store and manage files in the cloud. By leveraging the right storage solution, businesses can optimize their data management, enhance collaboration, and scale efficiently as their needs grow.

CHAPTER 9

NETWORKING IN THE CLOUD

Cloud networking forms the backbone of any cloud infrastructure, allowing resources to communicate securely, efficiently, and reliably. Whether you're building a web application, running a virtual private network (VPN), or managing multiple cloud services, understanding cloud networking fundamentals like **Virtual Private Cloud (VPC)**, **subnets**, and **VPNs** is essential. In this chapter, we'll explore these key concepts, how they work together, and how to create a secure network setup in **AWS** and **Azure**.

Cloud Networking Fundamentals

1. Virtual Private Cloud (VPC)

What **it** **is**:
A **Virtual Private Cloud (VPC)** is a logically isolated network within a cloud provider's environment where users can launch resources (like EC2 instances in AWS or Virtual Machines in Azure) and control the network configuration, such as IP addressing, subnets, route tables, and network gateways. A VPC allows users to create private, secure environments in the cloud

that function similarly to a traditional on-premises network but with the flexibility and scalability of the cloud.

How **it** **works**:
A VPC allows you to define your own private IP address range, subnets, and route tables. You can configure how different cloud resources communicate with each other and the outside world by managing inbound and outbound traffic rules. A VPC typically includes elements such as:

- **Subnets**: Dividing a VPC into smaller network segments.
- **Route Tables**: Defining how traffic is routed between subnets and to/from the internet.
- **Internet Gateway**: Connecting your VPC to the internet, enabling resources to access public services or be accessible from the internet.
- **NAT Gateway**: Allowing instances in a private subnet to initiate outbound traffic to the internet while preventing inbound traffic.

Benefits:

- **Isolation**: VPCs provide a private, secure network for your cloud resources.
- **Customization**: You can control the IP range, subnets, and routing to meet specific network design needs.

- **Security**: You can apply security rules at various levels (e.g., security groups, network ACLs) to control access to resources.

2. Subnets

What **it** **is**: A **subnet** is a segment of a VPC's IP address range where resources can be placed. Subnets allow you to organize your cloud resources by dividing your network into smaller, more manageable sections. Each subnet can be classified as either **public** or **private**, based on whether it requires access to the internet.

How it works:

- **Public Subnet**: Resources in a public subnet can directly communicate with the internet through the internet gateway (e.g., a web server or load balancer).
- **Private Subnet**: Resources in a private subnet do not have direct internet access. These subnets are typically used for databases, application servers, and other backend systems that need to be isolated from public traffic but still need to communicate with other resources in the cloud.

Benefits:

- **Network Organization**: Subnets allow for better organization and isolation of different types of workloads (e.g., separating web servers from databases).

- **Security**: By isolating sensitive resources (like databases) in private subnets, you can protect them from public access while allowing them to communicate with other services.

3. Virtual Private Network (VPN)

What **it** **is**:
A **VPN (Virtual Private Network)** allows secure communication between your on-premises network (or other cloud environments) and your cloud infrastructure over the public internet. VPNs create an encrypted tunnel that ensures data remains private and secure while it travels across the internet.

How **it** **works**:
VPNs in cloud environments typically rely on **IPsec (Internet Protocol Security)** for encryption and authentication. A VPN connection links an on-premises network to a VPC or connects multiple VPCs together in a **hybrid cloud** or **multi-cloud** setup. There are two main types of VPNs:

- **Site-to-Site VPN**: This connects an entire on-premises network to a VPC, typically used for hybrid cloud environments.

- **Client-to-Site VPN**: This allows individual users to securely connect to the cloud network from remote locations, typically used for remote workforce access.

Benefits:

- **Security**: VPNs encrypt data, preventing unauthorized access during transmission.
- **Private Communication**: VPNs allow secure communication between on-premises systems and cloud resources.
- **Cost-Effective**: VPNs provide a secure network connection without the need for expensive leased lines.

Connecting Different Parts of a Cloud Environment

Cloud environments often consist of multiple services and resources that need to communicate with each other, whether they are running on the same VPC or across different VPCs, regions, or even cloud providers. Here are several ways to connect different parts of your cloud environment:

1. Peering VPCs

- **What it is**: VPC peering allows two VPCs to connect and communicate privately. VPC peering can be used within the same cloud provider (e.g., AWS VPC peering, Azure VNet peering) or across different regions.

- **How it works**: Once two VPCs are peered, instances in both VPCs can communicate with each other using private IP addresses, as long as the correct routing and security policies are configured.

- **Benefits**: VPC peering is useful for multi-tier applications, connecting different regions, or integrating separate cloud environments.

2. Transit Gateway

- **What it is**: A **Transit Gateway** acts as a central hub to connect multiple VPCs, allowing them to communicate with each other through a central point. This simplifies network management by avoiding complex VPC peering configurations between multiple VPCs.

- **How it works**: The Transit Gateway allows different VPCs to communicate with one another via a central hub, making it easier to scale and manage inter-VPC communication.

- **Benefits**: Transit Gateway simplifies the network architecture and reduces the need for complex peer-to-peer connections across multiple VPCs.

3. Load Balancers

- **What it is**: A **load balancer** is used to distribute incoming traffic across multiple instances of a service, improving performance, availability, and fault tolerance.
- **How it works**: Load balancers can direct traffic based on various factors such as server health, availability, and response times. Both **Application Load Balancers (ALB)** and **Network Load Balancers (NLB)** are commonly used in cloud environments.
- **Benefits**: Load balancing ensures that traffic is evenly distributed across instances, preventing any single resource from becoming overwhelmed.

Example: Creating a Secure Network Setup in AWS or Azure

Now, let's walk through the process of setting up a secure network in **AWS** and **Azure**, covering the basics of VPC, subnets, and VPN configurations.

AWS – Creating a Secure Network Setup with VPC

1. **Create a VPC**:
   - In the AWS Management Console, go to the **VPC Dashboard** and click **Create VPC**.
   - Choose an IPv4 CIDR block (e.g., `10.0.0.0/16`) for your VPC and select the default settings for other options.

2. **Create Subnets**:
   - Create a **public subnet** (e.g., `10.0.1.0/24`) for resources that require internet access, such as a web server.
   - Create a **private subnet** (e.g., `10.0.2.0/24`) for resources like databases that don't need direct internet access.

3. **Set up an Internet Gateway**:
   - Attach an **Internet Gateway** to your VPC. This enables the public subnet to access the internet.
   - Update the route table for the public subnet to route traffic to the Internet Gateway.

4. **Create a VPN Connection**:
   - In the **VPN Connections** section, create a new VPN connection to link your on-premises network to your VPC.
   - Configure the VPN connection using IPsec and the necessary tunnel options.

5. **Security Groups and NACLs**:

   o Set up **security groups** to control inbound and outbound traffic to instances. For example, allow HTTP (port 80) access to your web server.

   o Use **Network ACLs (Access Control Lists)** to provide an additional layer of security at the subnet level.

Azure – Creating a Secure Network Setup with VNet

1. **Create a VNet**:

   o In the **Azure Portal**, go to **Virtual Networks** and click **Create**.

   o Define the VNet name and region, and select an IP address range (e.g., 10.0.0.0/16).

2. **Create Subnets**:

   o Add a **public subnet** (e.g., 10.0.1.0/24) for resources needing internet access.

   o Add a **private subnet** (e.g., 10.0.2.0/24) for backend services, such as databases.

3. **Set up a VPN Gateway**:

   o Create a **VPN Gateway** in the **Networking** section to establish secure communication between your on-premises network and Azure VNet.

98

- o Configure the VPN gateway with IPsec settings and create a **Connection** to the on-premises VPN device.

4. **Security Groups and NSGs**:
   - o Use **Network Security Groups (NSGs)** to define inbound and outbound traffic rules at the subnet or VM level.
   - o Apply **NSGs** to control which ports are open for incoming traffic (e.g., HTTP/HTTPS for web servers).

Conclusion

In this chapter, we explored essential cloud networking concepts such as **Virtual Private Cloud (VPC), subnets**, and **VPNs**. We also discussed the importance of connecting different parts of a cloud environment and how cloud providers offer tools like VPC peering, Transit Gateways, and Load Balancers to facilitate this. By following best practices for network segmentation and using secure methods like VPNs and firewalls, you can ensure that your cloud infrastructure remains both scalable and secure. The examples provided for **AWS** and **Azure** demonstrate how easy it is to set up a secure and functional network environment, whether you're building a single VPC or a more complex, hybrid cloud setup.

CHAPTER 10

CLOUD DATABASES AND DATA MANAGEMENT

Data management is a crucial aspect of any cloud infrastructure. Cloud databases, which are hosted and managed by cloud service providers, offer many advantages over traditional on-premise solutions. In this chapter, we will explore the different types of databases, focusing on the key differences between **SQL** and **NoSQL** databases. We will also discuss how cloud databases differ from on-premise databases and provide a practical example of setting up a **NoSQL database** using **AWS DynamoDB**.

Types of Databases (SQL vs. NoSQL)

1. SQL Databases

What **it** **is**:
SQL (Structured Query Language) databases, also known as **relational databases**, store data in tables with predefined schemas (columns and rows). They use SQL as the query language to interact with the data. SQL databases enforce a schema on data, meaning the data structure is defined before inserting the data into the database. Common examples of SQL databases include

100

MySQL, **PostgreSQL**, **Microsoft SQL Server**, and **Oracle Database**.

How it works:
In an SQL database, the data is stored in structured formats (tables) with a strict schema that defines data types, relationships between tables, and constraints. SQL databases are particularly suited for transactional applications that require ACID (Atomicity, Consistency, Isolation, Durability) compliance.

Benefits:

- **ACID Compliance**: SQL databases offer strong consistency and reliability, making them ideal for applications requiring transactional integrity (e.g., financial systems, e-commerce).
- **Structured Data**: SQL databases are best suited for applications where data follows a well-defined structure, such as customer information, orders, or inventory management.
- **Joins and Relationships**: SQL databases allow for complex queries using joins, enabling the creation of relationships between different tables.

2. NoSQL Databases

What it is:
NoSQL (Not Only SQL) databases are a family of databases that

provide a flexible and scalable alternative to traditional relational databases. They do not enforce a fixed schema and are designed to handle unstructured, semi-structured, or rapidly changing data. NoSQL databases are typically used in scenarios that require horizontal scaling and large volumes of data. Examples of NoSQL databases include **MongoDB**, **Cassandra**, **CouchDB**, and **AWS DynamoDB**.

How **it** **works**: NoSQL databases store data in various formats, including key-value pairs, document stores, column-family stores, and graph databases. They allow for flexible data models, making them ideal for applications with large, diverse, or frequently changing data. NoSQL databases typically scale out horizontally, meaning they distribute data across multiple nodes or servers, improving performance and scalability.

Benefits:

- **Scalability**: NoSQL databases are designed for horizontal scaling, making them ideal for handling big data and high-velocity applications.
- **Flexibility**: They allow for unstructured or semi-structured data, which is ideal for applications that deal with dynamic or rapidly changing data.
- **High Performance**: NoSQL databases provide fast read and write operations, especially for applications with

102

large-scale data like social media platforms, IoT, or real-time analytics.

Types of NoSQL Databases:

- **Key-Value Stores**: Stores data as a collection of key-value pairs (e.g., **Redis**, **DynamoDB**).
- **Document Stores**: Stores data as documents (e.g., **MongoDB**, **CouchDB**).
- **Column-Family Stores**: Stores data in columns rather than rows (e.g., **Apache Cassandra**).
- **Graph Databases**: Stores data as nodes and edges, ideal for representing relationships (e.g., **Neo4j**).

How Cloud Databases Differ from On-Premise Solutions

While both cloud databases and on-premise databases serve the same purpose—storing and managing data—they differ in several important ways, including infrastructure management, scalability, and cost-efficiency.

1. Infrastructure Management

- **Cloud Databases**: In a cloud environment, the cloud provider manages the underlying infrastructure, including hardware, software, maintenance, and scaling. The user only interacts with the database service via the cloud provider's interface.

- **On-Premise Databases**: On-premise databases are hosted on physical servers managed by the organization's IT team. This requires significant investment in hardware, data center facilities, and ongoing maintenance.

Benefits of Cloud Databases:

- **Managed Service**: Cloud databases are fully managed by the provider, meaning you don't need to worry about hardware, patches, backups, or scaling.
- **Elasticity**: Cloud databases can scale up or down quickly based on demand, allowing for more efficient use of resources.

2. Scalability

- **Cloud Databases**: Cloud databases are designed to scale horizontally. When traffic or data storage needs increase, the cloud provider can allocate more resources to meet demand, without requiring physical hardware upgrades. This allows businesses to easily scale their database infrastructure as their needs grow.

- **On-Premise Databases**: Scaling on-premise databases typically requires purchasing and installing new hardware, which can be expensive and time-consuming.

Benefits of Cloud Databases:

- **Horizontal Scaling**: Cloud databases can distribute workloads across multiple servers or regions, ensuring high availability and performance during peak demand.
- **Cost-Effective Scaling**: Instead of purchasing and maintaining extra hardware, businesses only pay for the resources they actually use.

3. Availability and Disaster Recovery

- **Cloud Databases**: Cloud providers offer built-in high availability and disaster recovery solutions, often replicating data across multiple regions or availability zones to ensure data is protected in case of failure.
- **On-Premise Databases**: On-premise solutions require manual configuration for redundancy and disaster recovery, which can be complex and expensive.

Benefits of Cloud Databases:

- **High Availability**: Cloud providers ensure that databases are available 24/7 with automated failover, minimizing downtime.

- **Built-in Backup and Recovery**: Cloud databases often include automated backups and disaster recovery tools, ensuring data is protected without manual intervention.

4. Cost

- **Cloud Databases**: Cloud databases are typically offered as a **pay-as-you-go** service, where users pay only for the storage, compute, and network resources they use. This allows businesses to avoid upfront hardware costs and focus on operational expenses.
- **On-Premise Databases**: On-premise databases require significant upfront capital investment in hardware, software licenses, and personnel for maintenance and management.

Benefits of Cloud Databases:

- **Cost Flexibility**: Cloud databases offer a cost-efficient model where users can scale up or down based on actual needs.
- **No Capital Expenditure**: With cloud databases, there's no need to purchase expensive hardware, as everything is managed by the cloud provider.

Example: Setting Up a NoSQL Database in AWS DynamoDB

Let's walk through the process of setting up a NoSQL database using **AWS DynamoDB**, a fully managed, key-value and document database service.

Step 1: Log into the AWS Management Console

1. Go to the **AWS Management Console** and sign in with your credentials.
2. In the search bar, type **DynamoDB** and select it from the results.

Step 2: Create a DynamoDB Table

1. In the DynamoDB console, click on **Create Table** to start the setup process.
2. **Table Name**: Enter a name for your table (e.g., `ProductsTable`).
3. **Primary Key**: DynamoDB requires a primary key. You can choose between a simple primary key (one partition key) or a composite primary key (partition key and sort key). For example, use `ProductID` as the partition key.
4. **Table Settings**: Leave the default settings for now, or you can modify them later based on your needs. DynamoDB

automatically scales to handle throughput, so you can set **Provisioned** or **On-demand** capacity.

5. Click **Create** to create the table.

Step 3: Add Data to DynamoDB

1. After the table is created, go to the **Items** tab and click **Create Item** to add data to your table.

2. Enter the **ProductID** and other attributes (e.g., ProductName, Price, etc.) and click **Save**.

Step 4: Query the Data

1. You can use the **Query** feature in the DynamoDB console to retrieve data from your table based on the ProductID or other attributes.

2. Click **Query** in the **Items** tab and specify the key or attribute you want to search for. DynamoDB will return the results quickly, showcasing its low-latency performance.

Step 5: Set Up Auto Scaling (Optional)

1. DynamoDB allows you to enable **auto scaling** to automatically adjust read and write capacity based on demand. In the **Table Settings**, you can configure **Auto Scaling** to handle changing workloads.

Conclusion

In this chapter, we explored the different types of databases, focusing on the differences between **SQL** and **NoSQL** databases. We also discussed how cloud databases, such as **AWS DynamoDB**, differ from traditional on-premise solutions in terms of scalability, management, cost, and availability. By leveraging cloud-based NoSQL databases, businesses can benefit from flexible, scalable, and cost-efficient data storage solutions that meet the demands of modern applications. The hands-on example of setting up a NoSQL database with **AWS DynamoDB** demonstrates how easy it is to get started with cloud databases and manage data in a cloud-native environment.

CHAPTER 11

DEPLOYING APPLICATIONS ON THE CLOUD

Cloud platforms have revolutionized the way applications are deployed, making it easier to manage, scale, and maintain applications. Deploying an application on the cloud eliminates the need to maintain physical servers and provides a wealth of tools for managing infrastructure, networking, and scalability. In this chapter, we will cover how to deploy a simple web application to the cloud, discuss deployment strategies for both **monolithic** and **microservice-based applications**, and provide a hands-on example by deploying a **Node.js app on Heroku**.

How to Deploy a Simple Web Application in the Cloud

Deploying a web application in the cloud typically involves several steps, from selecting a cloud platform to configuring the deployment environment and scaling the application. Here's a high-level overview of the process:

110

1. Choose a Cloud Provider

First, you need to choose a cloud provider based on your needs. For example, **AWS**, **Google Cloud**, **Azure**, or platforms like **Heroku** and **DigitalOcean** are all popular choices for deploying web applications. Depending on the complexity and needs of your application, you might choose a platform-as-a-service (PaaS) like Heroku for simplicity or an infrastructure-as-a-service (IaaS) solution like AWS EC2 for more control.

2. Set Up Your Cloud Environment

Once you've chosen your cloud provider, you'll need to create an environment for your application:

- **Virtual Machines or Containers**: For traditional server-based applications, deploy your app to a virtual machine (VM). For containerized applications, use services like **Docker** or **Kubernetes**.
- **Databases**: Set up any databases your app needs (e.g., **AWS RDS**, **Google Cloud SQL**, or **MongoDB Atlas** for NoSQL databases).
- **Networking**: Set up network configurations, such as firewalls, load balancers, and private subnets, depending on your application's requirements.

3. Configure the Deployment Environment

- Install dependencies and configure environment variables that your application needs to run (e.g., **Node.js**, **Python**, **Ruby**, etc.).
- Set up storage (e.g., file storage with **AWS S3**, **Azure Blob Storage**).

4. Deploy the Application

- **Push Code**: For most cloud platforms, you push your code to a version control system like **Git** (e.g., via **GitHub**, **GitLab**, or **Bitbucket**).
- **CI/CD Pipeline**: Set up a Continuous Integration/Continuous Deployment (CI/CD) pipeline to automate the deployment process (using tools like **Jenkins**, **GitLab CI**, **AWS CodePipeline**).
- **Manual Deployment**: For platforms that don't have CI/CD support, deploy your code manually via command-line tools or through the cloud platform's interface.

5. Monitor and Scale

- **Scaling**: Depending on traffic or resource usage, you can scale your application by adding more servers or resources, either manually or using auto-scaling.

112

- **Monitoring**: Use cloud monitoring tools (e.g., **AWS CloudWatch**, **Google Stackdriver**, or **Datadog**) to track performance and resource utilization.

Deploying Both Monolithic and Microservice-Based Apps

1. Monolithic Application Deployment

A **monolithic application** is a traditional software architecture where all parts of the application (front end, back end, database, etc.) are integrated into a single package or module. This approach works well for small to medium-sized applications but may face challenges as the application grows in complexity.

Steps to deploy a monolithic application in the cloud:

- **Prepare the App**: Bundle all parts of the application together, ensuring everything works seamlessly as a single unit.
- **Choose a Deployment Option**: Depending on the cloud provider, you can deploy your monolithic app to a **virtual machine** (e.g., **AWS EC2, Azure VM**), or to a **Platform-as-a-Service (PaaS)** like **Heroku** or **AWS Elastic**

Beanstalk, which abstracts much of the infrastructure management.

- **Scale Manually or Horizontally**: While a monolithic app can be scaled by adding more instances (horizontal scaling), this can become inefficient as the app grows.

2. Microservice-Based Application Deployment

A **microservice-based application** is a more modern architecture where the application is broken down into smaller, loosely coupled services, each responsible for a specific piece of functionality. These services communicate with each other via APIs.

Steps to deploy a microservice-based application in the cloud:

- **Containerization**: Use **Docker** to containerize each microservice, ensuring they can be deployed and managed independently.
- **Orchestration**: Deploy the containers using an **orchestration platform** like **Kubernetes** or **AWS ECS** (Elastic Container Service) to manage multiple services, scaling, and load balancing.
- **APIs and Service Communication**: Ensure that each microservice communicates with others via APIs or messaging queues (e.g., **RabbitMQ**, **Kafka**).

114

- **Service Discovery**: Use a service discovery mechanism to ensure that services can dynamically find and communicate with one another.

Example: Deploying a Node.js App on Heroku

Heroku is one of the most user-friendly cloud platforms for deploying web applications, especially for small projects or rapid prototyping. In this example, we will walk through deploying a simple **Node.js** web application on Heroku.

Step 1: Set Up Heroku Account and CLI

1. **Create a Heroku Account**: Go to Heroku and sign up for a free account.
2. **Install Heroku CLI**: Download and install the Heroku CLI (Command Line Interface) from Heroku CLI.
3. **Log In**: Open your terminal or command prompt and log in to Heroku by typing:

bash

```
heroku login
```

Step 2: Prepare Your Node.js Application

1. **Create a Node.js App**: If you don't already have a Node.js app, create a simple app using Express.js. Here's a simple example:

bash

```bash
mkdir my-node-app
cd my-node-app
npm init -y
npm install express
```

2. **Create index.js**:

javascript

```javascript
const express = require('express');
const app = express();
const port = process.env.PORT || 3000;

app.get('/', (req, res) => {
  res.send('Hello World!');
});

app.listen(port, () => {
  console.log(`App        listening       at
http://localhost:${port}`);
});
```

3. **Create `package.json`**: Ensure your `package.json` file has the proper start script for Heroku:

```json
json

{
  "name": "my-node-app",
  "version": "1.0.0",
  "main": "index.js",
  "scripts": {
    "start": "node index.js"
  },
  "dependencies": {
    "express": "^4.17.1"
  }
}
```

Step 3: Initialize Git and Push Code

1. **Initialize Git**: In your app folder, run the following commands to initialize Git and create a repository:

```bash
bash

git init
git add .
git commit -m "Initial commit"
```

2. **Create a Heroku App**: In the terminal, run the following command to create a new app on Heroku:

117

```
bash
```

```
heroku create
```

This will create a new Heroku app with a random name and a corresponding Git remote (`heroku`).

3. **Deploy the App**: Push your code to Heroku:

```
bash
```

```
git push heroku master
```

Heroku will automatically detect that it's a Node.js application and will set up the necessary environment to run it.

Step 4: Access Your Application

After the deployment is complete, Heroku will provide a URL where you can access your app:

```
bash
```

```
https://your-app-name.herokuapp.com
```

Visit the URL in your browser to see the "Hello World!" message.

Conclusion

In this chapter, we explored how to deploy both **monolithic** and **microservice-based** applications in the cloud, with a focus on different deployment strategies and cloud platforms. We also walked through a hands-on example of deploying a **Node.js** app on **Heroku**, demonstrating how cloud platforms simplify the process of hosting and scaling applications. By leveraging cloud-based deployment solutions, developers can quickly get their applications into production, ensuring reliability, scalability, and ease of management. As you continue to build cloud-based applications, you'll encounter even more powerful deployment and management tools to help automate processes and scale efficiently.

CHAPTER 12

AUTOMATING WITH CLOUD SERVICES

As cloud environments grow in complexity, automation becomes an essential tool for managing and scaling infrastructure. Cloud automation tools help streamline repetitive tasks, reduce human error, and ensure consistency in cloud resource management. In this chapter, we will explore popular cloud automation tools such as **CloudFormation** and **Terraform**, discuss how automation helps with scaling and management, and provide a hands-on example of automating infrastructure with **Terraform**.

Introduction to Cloud Automation Tools

Cloud automation tools are designed to automate the deployment, management, and scaling of infrastructure in cloud environments. These tools allow you to define and manage your cloud infrastructure as code, making it easier to replicate environments, manage resources consistently, and reduce the potential for manual configuration errors.

1. AWS CloudFormation

What it is:
AWS CloudFormation is a service that allows you to define and provision AWS infrastructure using a declarative template. CloudFormation templates are written in **JSON** or **YAML** and describe the cloud resources and their configurations. Once the template is created, CloudFormation automates the process of provisioning and managing the resources.

How it works:

- You define your infrastructure in a **CloudFormation template** (e.g., EC2 instances, VPCs, security groups).
- You create a **CloudFormation stack**, which is a collection of AWS resources defined in the template.
- CloudFormation automatically provisions and configures the resources for you.

Benefits:

- **Consistency**: CloudFormation ensures that your infrastructure is deployed consistently across different environments.
- **Declarative**: You describe the desired end state (e.g., a specific EC2 instance configuration), and CloudFormation handles the details of resource creation.

121

- **Version Control**: CloudFormation templates can be versioned, allowing you to track and manage changes to your infrastructure.

2. Terraform

What it is: Terraform is an open-source tool developed by **HashiCorp** that allows you to define, provision, and manage infrastructure across multiple cloud providers using a high-level configuration language known as **HCL (HashiCorp Configuration Language)**. Unlike CloudFormation, which is AWS-specific, Terraform is multi-cloud and can manage resources across AWS, Azure, Google Cloud, and many other providers.

How it works:

- You write **Terraform configuration files** in HCL that define your infrastructure (e.g., compute resources, databases, networking).
- Terraform uses a **state file** to track the current state of the infrastructure and compare it to the desired state defined in the configuration files.
- When you run **terraform apply**, Terraform automatically provisions or modifies the resources to match the desired state.

Benefits:

- **Multi-Cloud Support**: Terraform can manage infrastructure across multiple cloud providers, enabling consistent configuration management.
- **Modular**: Terraform allows you to create reusable modules, which makes it easier to define common patterns for infrastructure deployment.
- **State Management**: Terraform maintains the state of your infrastructure, which helps with tracking and troubleshooting changes.

How Automation Helps with Scaling and Management

Automation in the cloud significantly enhances how infrastructure is managed and scaled. Here are several ways cloud automation tools help with scaling and management:

1. Efficient Resource Provisioning

- **Automated Deployment**: Cloud automation tools eliminate manual provisioning of resources, reducing the risk of human error. With a defined template or configuration, resources are automatically created in the correct environment.

- **Rapid Deployment**: Once templates or configuration files are written, deploying infrastructure becomes as easy as running a single command. This speeds up the process of setting up cloud environments, whether for development, testing, or production.

2. Consistency Across Environments

- **Infrastructure as Code**: Cloud automation tools enable the concept of **Infrastructure as Code (IaC)**, which means that your infrastructure is managed and versioned like application code. This ensures that environments are consistent and reduces configuration drift.
- **Replicability**: You can replicate environments easily by reusing templates or configuration files. This is particularly useful for scaling applications or replicating environments in different regions.

3. Automated Scaling

- **Elasticity**: Cloud automation tools can automatically scale resources up or down based on defined parameters. For example, **Terraform** can be used to create scaling policies that adjust the number of instances in response to traffic changes. **CloudFormation** can automate the creation of auto-scaling groups to ensure that resources are added or removed based on demand.

- **Cost Optimization**: Automation helps ensure that resources are only used when needed. By automatically scaling down unused resources, businesses can save on costs.

4. Continuous Integration and Delivery (CI/CD)

- **Infrastructure Automation in CI/CD**: Cloud automation can be integrated with CI/CD pipelines, enabling continuous deployment of applications and infrastructure updates. Automation ensures that changes to the infrastructure are deployed consistently and without error.

5. Simplified Management

- **Automated Updates and Patches**: Cloud automation tools can be used to apply updates or patches to infrastructure automatically, ensuring that systems are always up-to-date without manual intervention.
- **Centralized Management**: Automation allows for the central management of infrastructure across multiple cloud providers or environments, making it easier to maintain control and monitor performance.

Example: Automating Infrastructure with Terraform

In this section, we will walk through the steps of using **Terraform** to automate the deployment of infrastructure on AWS. For simplicity, we will set up an EC2 instance in AWS.

Step 1: Install Terraform

1. Download and install Terraform from the official Terraform website.
2. Verify the installation by running the following command in your terminal:

```bash

terraform -v
```

This should return the version of Terraform installed.

Step 2: Create a Terraform Configuration File

1. Create a new directory for your project:

```bash

mkdir my-terraform-project
cd my-terraform-project
```

2. Inside the project directory, create a new file named main.tf with the following content:

```hcl
provider "aws" {
  region = "us-east-1"
}

resource "aws_instance" "example" {
  ami             = "ami-0c55b159cbfafe1f0"
# Replace with the correct AMI ID for your region
  instance_type = "t2.micro"

  tags = {
    Name = "MyTerraformInstance"
  }
}
```

In this configuration:

- o We define the AWS provider and set the region to us-east-1.
- o We create an EC2 instance with the specified **AMI ID** and **instance type** (t2.micro).

Step 3: Initialize Terraform

1. Initialize the project directory by running:

    ```bash
    ```

    ```bash
    terraform init
    ```

    This command downloads the necessary provider plugins for Terraform.

Step 4: Plan the Deployment

1. Run the `terraform plan` command to see what changes Terraform will make:

    ```bash
    ```

    ```bash
    terraform plan
    ```

    Terraform will output a list of actions it will take, such as creating an EC2 instance.

Step 5: Apply the Configuration

1. Apply the configuration to create the EC2 instance:

    ```bash
    ```

    ```bash
    terraform apply
    ```

128

Terraform will prompt you to confirm the actions. Type `yes` to proceed.

Terraform will automatically provision the EC2 instance based on the configuration provided.

Step 6: Verify the Deployment

1. Log into your AWS Management Console and navigate to the **EC2 Dashboard**. You should see the newly created EC2 instance listed with the **Name** tag set to `MyTerraformInstance`.

Step 7: Destroy the Infrastructure

1. When you are done, you can destroy the resources created by Terraform by running:

```bash
bash
```

```
terraform destroy
```

Terraform will prompt you to confirm that you want to delete the infrastructure. Type `yes` to destroy the resources.

Conclusion

In this chapter, we explored **cloud automation tools** like **AWS CloudFormation** and **Terraform**, which simplify the process of deploying and managing infrastructure in the cloud. We discussed how automation helps with scaling, management, and reducing manual errors. Through a hands-on example of **Terraform**, we demonstrated how easy it is to automate the creation of resources in the cloud. By using automation tools, businesses can deploy infrastructure more efficiently, maintain consistency across environments, and easily scale their applications as needed. As you continue to work with cloud environments, leveraging automation will be key to managing infrastructure and optimizing operations.

CHAPTER 13

CLOUD MONITORING AND PERFORMANCE OPTIMIZATION

Monitoring and optimizing cloud applications is essential for ensuring they perform efficiently, scale as needed, and maintain high availability. As cloud environments are dynamic and often involve a variety of resources (e.g., virtual machines, databases, load balancers), effective monitoring tools and performance optimization strategies are necessary to ensure that applications meet user expectations. In this chapter, we will cover key **tools and strategies for monitoring cloud applications**, discuss **how to optimize performance**, and provide a practical example using **AWS CloudWatch** to monitor application performance.

Tools and Strategies for Monitoring Cloud Applications

1. Cloud Monitoring Tools

Effective cloud monitoring requires the use of specialized tools that track system performance, identify potential issues, and provide actionable insights. Most cloud service providers offer built-in monitoring tools that integrate directly with their platforms.

AWS CloudWatch

What **it** **is**: **AWS CloudWatch** is a monitoring service for AWS cloud resources and applications. It provides real-time monitoring for metrics such as CPU utilization, memory usage, network traffic, and disk I/O. CloudWatch also offers log collection, custom metrics, and the ability to create alarms based on defined thresholds.

Key Features:

- **Metrics**: CloudWatch collects and tracks metrics from AWS services like EC2, RDS, and Lambda. Metrics can also be collected from custom sources.
- **Logs**: CloudWatch Logs allows you to collect and store logs from your applications and AWS resources, making it easy to monitor logs and troubleshoot issues.
- **Alarms**: You can set CloudWatch Alarms to notify you when certain thresholds are met (e.g., CPU utilization exceeding 80%).
- **Dashboards**: CloudWatch provides customizable dashboards to visualize the performance metrics of your AWS resources in real-time.

132

Azure Monitor

What it is: **Azure Monitor** provides a comprehensive monitoring solution for applications and resources running on Microsoft Azure. It allows you to collect, analyze, and act on telemetry data from Azure services, applications, and virtual machines.

Key Features:

- **Application Insights**: This is a feature of Azure Monitor that provides detailed insights into the performance, availability, and usage of your applications.
- **Metrics and Logs**: Azure Monitor collects both metrics and logs from Azure resources, helping you track and manage performance.
- **Alerts and Notifications**: Azure Monitor allows you to set up alerts based on specific performance metrics and resource usage thresholds.

Google Cloud Operations Suite (formerly Stackdriver)

What it is: **Google Cloud Operations Suite** (formerly known as Stackdriver) is a set of tools for monitoring, logging, and tracing applications running on Google Cloud. It helps developers ensure that their applications run efficiently, perform well, and remain highly available.

Key Features:

- **Metrics and Dashboards**: Provides detailed metrics on Google Cloud resources and services.
- **Logging and Error Reporting**: Collects logs from Google Cloud applications and provides error reporting for easy debugging.
- **Tracing**: Helps visualize and trace the performance of requests as they travel through different services.

2. Key Strategies for Monitoring Cloud Applications

1. Collect Real-Time Metrics

Monitoring real-time metrics is essential to understanding how well your cloud-hosted applications are performing. Key metrics to monitor include:

- **CPU Usage**: High CPU usage can indicate performance bottlenecks or overutilization of resources.
- **Memory Usage**: High memory usage can lead to slowdowns or application crashes.
- **Disk I/O**: Monitoring disk read/write performance can help identify storage-related issues.
- **Network Traffic**: Excessive network traffic can indicate issues such as DDoS attacks or misconfigured networking components.

- **Error Rates**: Track the rate of errors generated by your application to identify potential issues before they affect users.

2. Set Up Alarms and Alerts

Setting up alarms based on thresholds for key performance metrics ensures you are notified when something goes wrong. For example:

- **CPU Utilization Alarm**: Set an alarm to notify you when CPU usage exceeds a certain percentage (e.g., 85%) for a prolonged period.
- **Memory Usage Alarm**: Set an alarm to notify you if memory usage exceeds a certain threshold, indicating the need for scaling or optimization.
- **Error Rate Alarm**: An increase in error rates may indicate problems with your application code or infrastructure that need to be addressed immediately.

3. Log Collection and Analysis

Cloud logging services (such as **CloudWatch Logs**, **Azure Logs**, or **Google Cloud Logging**) allow you to collect, store, and analyze log data from your applications and resources. This data is crucial for troubleshooting and identifying performance issues.

- **Application Logs**: Collect logs from your application to track errors, performance bottlenecks, and unusual behavior.
- **Resource Logs**: Collect logs from cloud resources (e.g., EC2 instances, RDS databases) to monitor system events, crashes, and performance issues.

4. Use Dashboards for Visualization

Most cloud monitoring tools allow you to create **custom dashboards** to visualize the health of your cloud infrastructure. Dashboards help you monitor multiple metrics at once and make informed decisions based on real-time data. For instance:

- Use dashboards to display **CPU**, **memory**, and **disk usage** metrics for your EC2 instances or virtual machines.
- Create application-specific dashboards to visualize **response times**, **error rates**, and **user activity**.

How to Optimize the Performance of Cloud-Hosted Applications

Cloud performance optimization involves identifying and addressing potential bottlenecks in the application, infrastructure, and resources. Here are some strategies for optimizing cloud-hosted applications:

1. Autoscaling and Load Balancing

- **Autoscaling**: Autoscaling allows your application to automatically adjust the number of running instances or containers based on demand. This ensures that the application performs well during peak traffic times while avoiding resource overprovisioning during off-peak times.
  - o In **AWS**, use **Auto Scaling Groups** to automatically add or remove EC2 instances.
  - o In **Azure**, use **Virtual Machine Scale Sets** to automatically scale resources.
- **Load Balancing**: Load balancing distributes incoming traffic across multiple instances to ensure high availability and optimize performance. Use cloud load balancers to prevent any single server from becoming overwhelmed by traffic.
  - o **AWS** offers **Elastic Load Balancing (ELB)**.
  - o **Azure** offers **Azure Load Balancer**.
  - o **Google Cloud** offers **Cloud Load Balancing**.

2. Caching

Implement caching to store frequently accessed data in memory, reducing the time it takes to fetch that data from databases or external services. This can significantly improve the performance of web applications and reduce database load.

- Use **Amazon ElastiCache** or **Azure Cache for Redis** to implement caching.
- Set up content delivery networks (CDNs), like **Amazon CloudFront** or **Azure CDN**, to cache static content at edge locations for faster access.

3. Database Optimization

Database performance is crucial for the overall performance of cloud applications. Here are some database optimization techniques:

- **Indexing**: Ensure that your database queries are optimized by creating appropriate indexes.
- **Database Sharding**: Distribute large datasets across multiple databases (shards) to ensure faster read and write operations.
- **Read Replicas**: Use read replicas to offload read-heavy queries from the primary database and improve performance.

4. Optimize Code and Application Performance

- **Code Profiling**: Use application performance monitoring (APM) tools (e.g., **New Relic**, **Datadog**, **Azure Application Insights**) to profile your application and identify slow functions or areas for optimization.
- **Database Query Optimization**: Ensure that your queries are efficient by using proper indexing, limiting results, and avoiding unnecessary joins.
- **Content Compression**: Compress static content (e.g., images, CSS, JavaScript) to reduce bandwidth and improve load times.

5. Network Optimization

Optimize the network layer to ensure low-latency connections and minimal packet loss:

- Use **Direct Connect** (AWS) or **ExpressRoute** (Azure) to establish dedicated, high-speed connections between on-premises networks and the cloud.
- Implement **TCP Optimizations** for applications that use high-latency or unreliable networks.

Example: Using AWS CloudWatch to Monitor App Performance

Let's walk through the process of setting up **AWS CloudWatch** to monitor the performance of a Node.js application running on an **EC2 instance**.

Step 1: Set Up CloudWatch Monitoring

1. **Log in to AWS Console** and navigate to the **CloudWatch Dashboard**.
2. **Create Alarms** for key metrics such as **CPU utilization**, **memory usage**, and **disk I/O**.
   - o Go to **CloudWatch > Alarms > Create Alarm**.
   - o Select a metric (e.g., **EC2 > Per-Instance Metrics > CPUUtilization**) and set a threshold (e.g., CPU utilization exceeds 80% for 5 minutes).
3. **Create a Notification** to send an email or text message when the alarm is triggered.

Step 2: Set Up CloudWatch Logs

1. **Install the CloudWatch Logs Agent** on your EC2 instance:

```bash
```

```
sudo yum install awslogs
sudo service awslogs start
```

2. **Configure the logs agent** to send application logs (e.g., from **Node.js** or **Nginx**) to CloudWatch Logs by editing the /etc/awslogs/awslogs.conf file.

3. Verify that the logs are appearing in the **CloudWatch Logs** section.

Step 3: Create a CloudWatch Dashboard

1. **Go to CloudWatch Dashboards** and create a new dashboard.

2. Add widgets to the dashboard to visualize the metrics you are monitoring (e.g., CPU utilization, memory usage, application logs).

3. Use the dashboard to monitor your app's performance in real-time.

Conclusion

In this chapter, we covered the tools and strategies used for **monitoring cloud applications** and **optimizing performance**. We explored cloud monitoring services like **AWS CloudWatch**, **Azure Monitor**, and **Google Cloud Operations Suite**, and discussed how they help track performance metrics, logs, and resource utilization. We also provided best practices for scaling, optimizing code, and managing resources effectively. The example of using **AWS CloudWatch** demonstrated how easy it is to set up monitoring and alarms to ensure that your cloud-hosted applications perform at their best. By leveraging these monitoring tools and optimization techniques, you can ensure your cloud applications remain high-performing, reliable, and cost-efficient.

CHAPTER 14

CLOUD COST MANAGEMENT AND OPTIMIZATION

Managing cloud costs is one of the most critical aspects of operating in the cloud. While cloud services offer flexibility, scalability, and efficiency, they can also lead to unexpected expenses if not monitored and optimized. In this chapter, we will explore how cloud providers charge for services, discuss techniques for optimizing cloud costs, and provide a hands-on example using **AWS Cost Explorer** to manage and optimize cloud expenses.

How Cloud Providers Charge for Services

Cloud providers use various pricing models to charge for their services. Understanding these pricing structures is crucial for managing costs effectively.

1. Pay-as-You-Go (On-Demand)

What **it** **is**:
With pay-as-you-go pricing, you are charged based on your actual usage of cloud resources, such as computing power, storage, and

network bandwidth. There are no upfront costs, and you are billed based on the resources you consume.

How it works:

- You are billed for the number of hours a server runs, the amount of storage used, or the data transferred out of the cloud.
- For example, in **AWS EC2**, you pay for the instances you launch based on the instance type and the time they are running.

Benefits:

- **Cost Flexibility**: You only pay for what you use, making it ideal for businesses with fluctuating demand.
- **No Upfront Commitment**: You can start small and scale as needed without making large upfront investments.

2. Reserved Instances (Long-Term Commitment)

What   it   is:
Reserved instances are a pricing model in which you commit to using a specific amount of cloud resources (such as virtual machines or database instances) for a fixed period (typically one or three years). In exchange for the commitment, you receive a discount on the hourly rates compared to on-demand pricing.

How it works:

- You select a resource type (e.g., EC2 instance) and reserve it for a fixed term.
- For example, **AWS EC2 Reserved Instances** offer savings of up to 75% compared to on-demand pricing when you commit to a one- or three-year term.

Benefits:

- **Cost Savings**: Reserved instances offer significant discounts over on-demand pricing.
- **Predictable Costs**: With long-term commitment, you can more accurately forecast and budget your cloud expenses.

3. Spot Instances (Excess Capacity)

What **it** **is**: Spot instances allow you to purchase unused cloud capacity at a discounted rate. These instances can be terminated by the cloud provider with little notice, so they are best suited for non-critical, flexible workloads.

How it works:

- **AWS EC2 Spot Instances**, for example, let you bid for unused EC2 capacity. If your bid is higher than the current spot price, you are allocated the instance at a fraction of the cost of on-demand pricing.

Benefits:

- **Cost-Effective**: Spot instances can offer significant savings (up to 90% off on-demand pricing).
- **Ideal for Flexible Workloads**: Perfect for batch processing, data analysis, or applications that can tolerate interruptions.

4. Subscription and Usage-Based Pricing

What   it   is: Some cloud services are billed based on subscription models, where you pay a flat fee for access to a particular service over a set period. Others charge based on the usage of specific features or data (e.g., data storage, network bandwidth).

How it works:

- **Azure Storage** charges based on the amount of data stored and the type of storage (e.g., Blob Storage, Disk Storage).
- **Google Cloud Storage** charges based on the amount of data stored and the frequency of access (e.g., Standard, Nearline, Coldline storage).

Benefits:

- **Predictable Pricing**: Subscription-based models offer predictable costs.
- **Granular Billing**: Usage-based pricing allows you to only pay for what you use, avoiding paying for unused resources.

Techniques to Optimize Cloud Costs

Optimizing cloud costs is essential to ensure that you're getting the most value out of your cloud resources. Here are some key techniques for managing and optimizing cloud spending:

1. Right-Sizing Resources

What **it** **is**:
Right-sizing involves adjusting the size of your cloud resources (e.g., EC2 instances, databases) to match the actual demand. Over-provisioning leads to wasted costs, while under-provisioning can lead to performance issues.

How it works:

- Regularly monitor resource usage (e.g., CPU, memory, storage) to identify over-provisioned instances.

147

- Use tools like **AWS Compute Optimizer** or **Azure Advisor** to get recommendations for instance types based on your usage patterns.

Benefits:

- **Cost Efficiency**: By ensuring you are only using the resources you need, you can avoid unnecessary costs.
- **Improved Performance**: Right-sizing helps avoid bottlenecks caused by undersized resources.

2. Auto-Scaling

What **it** **is**:
Auto-scaling allows you to automatically adjust the number of cloud instances (e.g., EC2, Virtual Machines) based on demand. This means you only use the resources you need at any given time.

How it works:

- Set up auto-scaling policies based on metrics like CPU utilization, memory usage, or request rates.
- For example, AWS **Auto Scaling** and **Elastic Load Balancer (ELB)** automatically add or remove instances based on demand, ensuring that you don't over-provision resources during low-traffic periods.

Benefits:

- **Cost Savings**: Auto-scaling ensures you're not paying for unused resources, automatically reducing costs during off-peak times.
- **Flexibility**: Your infrastructure can grow or shrink dynamically as needed, maintaining application performance without overpaying.

3. Leverage Reserved Instances and Savings Plans

What it is: When your workloads are predictable, committing to **Reserved Instances** or **Savings Plans** (AWS) can offer substantial savings over on-demand pricing.

How it works:

- For example, with **AWS Savings Plans**, you commit to a certain level of compute usage (e.g., a certain amount of EC2 usage) in exchange for up to 72% savings compared to on-demand pricing.
- **Azure Reserved Virtual Machine Instances** work similarly, providing discounts for committing to one or three years of usage.

Benefits:

- **Significant Savings**: Commit to long-term usage and enjoy discounts for up to three years.

149

- **Predictable Costs**: Lock in predictable costs for your resources, which simplifies budgeting and cost forecasting.

4. Optimize Storage Costs

What   it   is:
Cloud storage pricing can be optimized by choosing the right storage tier based on your data access patterns. For example, not all data needs to be stored in high-performance storage.

How it works:

- Use different storage classes (e.g., **AWS S3 Standard**, **S3 Glacier** for archival data) to ensure that data is stored at the lowest cost for the required access speed.
- Regularly audit your storage usage to identify and move unused or infrequently accessed data to lower-cost storage tiers.

Benefits:

- **Cost Reduction**: Move data that's not actively used to cheaper storage options.
- **Efficient Data Management**: By using tiered storage, you can optimize both cost and performance based on your application needs.

5. Monitor and Analyze Cloud Spending

What it is: Regularly monitor and analyze your cloud spending to identify trends and potential areas for savings. Cloud providers offer detailed billing reports and tools to help you track costs.

How it works:

- Use tools like **AWS Cost Explorer**, **Google Cloud Billing**, or **Azure Cost Management** to track and visualize your cloud spending. Set up cost and usage reports to identify underutilized resources.
- Regularly review and refine your cloud spending strategy to ensure that you are always using the most cost-effective resources for your needs.

Benefits:

- **Transparency**: Understanding where your cloud spending is going allows you to make data-driven decisions about where to optimize.
- **Proactive Cost Management**: Ongoing monitoring helps you identify potential cost overruns and take action before they become significant issues.

Example: Cost Management Using AWS Cost Explorer

AWS Cost Explorer is a powerful tool that allows you to visualize, track, and manage your cloud spending. Here's how to use it to optimize your AWS costs.

Step 1: Access Cost Explorer

1. Log in to the **AWS Management Console**.
2. Navigate to **Billing and Cost Management** and select **Cost Explorer** under the **Cost Management** section.

Step 2: Set Up Cost and Usage Reports

1. **Filter by Service**: You can filter the data to view costs for specific AWS services (e.g., EC2, S3, RDS).
2. **Time Range**: Set the time range for the report (e.g., monthly, weekly, or custom date ranges).
3. **View Recommendations**: AWS Cost Explorer provides recommendations for rightsizing your resources and switching to Reserved Instances based on your usage patterns.

Step 3: Identify Trends and Inefficiencies

1. Use the **Cost Explorer Dashboard** to visualize your cloud spending over time and identify any significant increases.

2. Look for underutilized resources, such as EC2 instances with low CPU utilization, and consider downsizing or terminating them to save costs.

Step 4: Set Up Alerts

1. Set up **AWS Budgets** to alert you when your cloud spending exceeds a certain threshold.

2. You can create custom alerts for specific services to keep track of any unexpected spikes in usage.

Step 5: Optimize Costs

1. After identifying areas where costs can be optimized, take action to right-size instances, move unused data to cheaper storage, or switch to Reserved Instances.

Conclusion

In this chapter, we covered the essential aspects of **cloud cost management and optimization**. We discussed how cloud providers charge for services, including **pay-as-you-go**, **reserved instances**, and **spot instances**. We explored several strategies to optimize cloud costs, such as **right-sizing**, **auto-scaling**, **leveraging reserved instances**, and **optimizing storage**. Additionally, we walked through a practical example using **AWS Cost Explorer** to manage cloud spending. By understanding and implementing these strategies, you can effectively manage your cloud costs while ensuring that your applications run efficiently and scale as needed.

CHAPTER 15

SERVERLESS COMPUTING

Serverless computing is a cloud model that allows you to run applications and services without managing servers. In this chapter, we will explore the serverless computing model, discuss when to use serverless services like **AWS Lambda**, and provide a hands-on example of building a serverless function using **AWS Lambda**.

Understanding the Serverless Model

What is Serverless Computing?

Serverless computing is a cloud computing model where the cloud provider automatically manages the infrastructure. You don't need to worry about provisioning, scaling, or maintaining servers. Instead, you can focus on writing and deploying code in the form of functions or services that are executed in response to events, such as HTTP requests, file uploads, or database changes.

In the serverless model, the cloud provider automatically allocates resources, handles scaling, and ensures high availability. You only pay for the compute time you use, making serverless computing highly cost-effective for certain types of workloads.

How It Works:

- **Function Execution**: In a serverless architecture, your application logic is written in the form of small, stateless functions that are triggered by events (e.g., HTTP requests, data changes).

- **Event-Driven**: Serverless functions are executed in response to specific events. For example, a function might be triggered when a new file is uploaded to cloud storage, or when a user submits a form on a website.

- **Automatic Scaling**: The serverless platform automatically scales the resources based on the number of incoming events. For example, if there are a lot of requests, the platform will automatically spin up more instances to handle the load, and scale down when traffic decreases.

- **No Server Management**: You don't need to manage or configure the underlying servers. The cloud provider abstracts away the infrastructure management tasks, freeing you to focus on your code.

Benefits of Serverless Computing:

- **Cost Efficiency**: With serverless, you pay only for the actual compute time used by your functions, meaning you're not paying for idle time.

- **Automatic Scaling**: Serverless functions scale automatically based on demand, ensuring that your application can handle large spikes in traffic without requiring manual intervention.
- **Simplified Operations**: You don't need to worry about server provisioning, maintenance, or scaling. This reduces operational overhead.
- **Faster Development**: Developers can focus on writing code and defining business logic, rather than managing servers or infrastructure.

When to Use Serverless Services Like AWS Lambda

While serverless computing offers many advantages, it is not the right choice for every use case. Here are some scenarios where serverless services like **AWS Lambda** shine:

1. Event-Driven Applications

Serverless computing is particularly useful for applications that are triggered by events. For example:

- **Real-time data processing**: You can process data as it flows into your system, such as processing log files, streaming data from IoT devices, or reacting to changes in a database.

- **HTTP Request Handlers**: You can use serverless functions to handle HTTP requests, making it easy to build RESTful APIs.

2. Microservices Architecture

Serverless is well-suited for building microservices because it allows you to decompose your application into small, manageable services that can be independently deployed and scaled. Each microservice can be implemented as a serverless function, making it easier to maintain and scale.

3. Short-Lived Tasks

Serverless functions are ideal for tasks that don't require a long time to complete. Examples include:

- **Image or video processing**: Convert images or videos when uploaded.
- **Data transformation**: Transform or validate incoming data streams or files.

4. Variable or Unpredictable Traffic

If your application experiences unpredictable traffic patterns or sudden spikes, serverless functions can automatically scale to accommodate the demand. For example, handling sudden bursts of requests during sales events or promotions.

5. Cost Efficiency for Low-Volume, Sporadic Workloads

If your application has periods of inactivity but needs to run sporadically (e.g., running a task once a day or month), serverless can be a cost-effective solution since you only pay for the function execution time.

6. Integration with Other Cloud Services

Serverless functions integrate well with other cloud services (e.g., cloud storage, messaging queues, databases). For example, AWS Lambda can be triggered by events in **Amazon S3**, **Amazon SNS**, or **Amazon DynamoDB**, making it ideal for building event-driven workflows.

Example: Building a Serverless Function with AWS Lambda

Let's walk through a simple example of building a serverless function using **AWS Lambda**. In this example, we will create a Lambda function that processes an image uploaded to **Amazon S3** by resizing it.

Step 1: Set Up Your AWS Account

1. Sign in to the **AWS Management Console**.

2. Navigate to **AWS Lambda** and make sure you have the necessary permissions to create Lambda functions and access other AWS services like S3.

Step 2: Create an S3 Bucket for Image Uploads

1. In the AWS Management Console, go to **S3** and create a new bucket (e.g., `my-image-bucket`).

2. Make sure to set appropriate permissions for the bucket to allow Lambda to access files.

Step 3: Create a Lambda Function

1. Go to the **Lambda** service in the AWS Management Console.

2. Click **Create Function**.
   - Choose **Author from Scratch**.
   - Name your function (e.g., `resize-image-function`).
   - Choose **Node.js** as the runtime (or another language if preferred).
   - Set the execution role to give Lambda permission to access your S3 bucket. You can create a new role with the

`AWSLambdaBasicExecutionRole` **and** `AmazonS3ReadOnlyAccess` policies.

Step 4: Write the Lambda Function Code

In the **Function Code** section, write the following code to resize images using the **Sharp** image processing library. You can upload libraries in the Lambda function by using **AWS Lambda Layers**.

```javascript
const AWS = require('aws-sdk');
const sharp = require('sharp');

const s3 = new AWS.S3();

exports.handler = async (event) => {
    const bucket = event.Records[0].s3.bucket.name;
    const key = decodeURIComponent(event.Records[0].s3.object.key.replace(/\+/g, ' '));

    try {
        const originalImage = await s3.getObject({ Bucket: bucket, Key: key }).promise();
```

161

```
      const      resizedImage      =      await
sharp(originalImage.Body)
          .resize(200, 200)
          .toBuffer();

      const resizedKey = 'resized-' + key;

      await s3.putObject({
          Bucket: bucket,
          Key: resizedKey,
          Body: resizedImage,
          ContentType: 'image/jpeg'
      }).promise();

      console.log(`Successfully   resized   and
uploaded image to ${resizedKey}`);

   } catch (error) {
      console.error(error);
      throw new Error('Error resizing image');
   }
};
```

- The code fetches the image from the S3 bucket using the `getObject` method.
- It uses the **Sharp** library to resize the image to 200x200 pixels.
- It then uploads the resized image to the same S3 bucket with a `resized-` prefix using the `putObject` method.

Step 5: Set Up the S3 Trigger

1. In the **Designer** section of your Lambda function, click on **Add Trigger** and select **S3**.
2. Choose the **S3 bucket** (`my-image-bucket`) and set the event type to **ObjectCreated**.
   o This will trigger the Lambda function every time a new image is uploaded to the S3 bucket.

Step 6: Test the Lambda Function

1. Upload an image (e.g., a JPEG file) to your **S3 bucket**.
2. Lambda will automatically trigger in response to the upload, resize the image, and upload it back to the bucket with the resized dimensions.

Step 7: Check the Results

1. In your **S3 bucket**, you should see the resized image with a name like `resized-your-image.jpg`.
2. You can also check the **CloudWatch Logs** to see any logs generated by your Lambda function.

Conclusion

In this chapter, we explored the **serverless computing model**, focusing on the advantages of using services like **AWS Lambda** for building scalable, event-driven applications without worrying about server management. We discussed when to use serverless services, including scenarios like event-driven processing, microservices, short-lived tasks, and variable traffic.

The hands-on example demonstrated how easy it is to create a serverless function with **AWS Lambda** to process images uploaded to an **S3 bucket**, showing the power and simplicity of serverless architectures. By adopting serverless computing, businesses can reduce operational overhead, achieve cost savings, and focus on building and deploying applications without managing infrastructure.

CHAPTER 16

CONTAINERS AND KUBERNETES

Containers and container orchestration have become the standard for deploying applications in the cloud. They offer a lightweight, efficient way to run software consistently across various environments. In this chapter, we will introduce the concept of **containers**, explain **Docker**, and dive into **Kubernetes** and how it helps with container orchestration. Finally, we'll walk through an example of deploying a containerized application using Kubernetes.

Introduction to Containers and Docker

What are Containers?

Containers are lightweight, standalone, executable packages that include everything needed to run a piece of software, including the code, runtime, libraries, and dependencies. Containers provide a consistent runtime environment, ensuring that the application behaves the same way on any system, whether it's a developer's local machine or a cloud server.

Key Features of Containers:

- **Isolation**: Containers provide a way to isolate applications from the underlying host system and other applications. Each container runs independently, reducing the risk of conflicts.

- **Portability**: Containers can run consistently across different environments, from local development machines to staging and production environments.

- **Efficiency**: Containers are lightweight compared to virtual machines, using fewer resources and providing faster startup times.

What is Docker?

Docker is the most popular containerization platform. It allows you to build, package, and distribute applications as containers. Docker provides a consistent way to manage containers across various environments.

Key Concepts in Docker:

- **Docker Images**: A Docker image is a read-only template used to create containers. Images define the application, libraries, dependencies, and configuration required to run the application.

- **Docker Containers**: A container is a running instance of a Docker image. It's isolated from the host system and other containers, but it can interact with the outside world via defined ports and volumes.

- **Dockerfile**: A Dockerfile is a script that contains a set of instructions to build a Docker image. It defines the base image, application dependencies, and configuration.

Benefits of Docker:

- **Consistency**: Docker ensures that an application runs consistently across various environments.
- **Isolation**: Applications running in containers are isolated from each other, preventing interference.
- **Versioning**: Docker images can be versioned, making it easy to roll back to previous versions of an application.

What Kubernetes Is and How It Helps with Container Orchestration

What is Kubernetes?

Kubernetes (often abbreviated as **K8s**) is an open-source container orchestration platform developed by Google. It helps automate the deployment, scaling, and management of containerized applications. While Docker manages individual containers, Kubernetes manages clusters of containers, ensuring that they run efficiently, are scaled appropriately, and remain healthy.

Key Concepts in Kubernetes:

- **Pod**: The smallest unit in Kubernetes. A pod is a group of one or more containers that are deployed together on the same node. Pods share the same network namespace and storage.
- **Node**: A node is a physical or virtual machine that runs containers in Kubernetes. It can be part of a Kubernetes cluster.
- **Cluster**: A collection of nodes managed by Kubernetes. A cluster provides high availability and can scale workloads as needed.
- **Deployment**: A deployment is a Kubernetes resource that manages the deployment of applications in pods, ensuring that the desired number of pod replicas is running at all times.
- **Service**: A service in Kubernetes provides a stable endpoint (IP address and port) to access a set of pods. It enables communication between different components of the application.
- **ReplicaSet**: A ReplicaSet ensures that a specific number of pod replicas are running at any given time, helping with scaling and ensuring high availability.

168

- **Namespace**: A namespace is a way to partition a Kubernetes cluster, enabling multiple teams or applications to share the same cluster while keeping their resources isolated.

Why Kubernetes?

Kubernetes is designed to:

- **Manage large-scale applications**: Kubernetes allows you to deploy, scale, and manage complex applications that consist of multiple containers.
- **Handle scalability and high availability**: Kubernetes automatically scales applications based on demand, ensuring high availability even if some containers fail.
- **Load balancing**: Kubernetes ensures that traffic is distributed evenly across all containers, improving performance and fault tolerance.
- **Automated rollouts and rollbacks**: Kubernetes allows you to automate application updates and rollbacks, making deployments easier and more reliable.
- **Self-healing**: Kubernetes monitors the health of containers and automatically restarts or reschedules them if they fail.

Example: Deploying a Containerized App Using Kubernetes

Let's walk through an example of deploying a containerized **Node.js** application using **Kubernetes**. We will use Docker to containerize the app and Kubernetes to manage the deployment, scaling, and operation of the application.

Step 1: Build a Docker Image for the Application

1. **Create the Node.js Application**:
   - Start by creating a simple **Node.js** application. Here's a basic example:

```javascript
// app.js
const http = require('http');

const requestListener = (req, res) => {
  res.writeHead(200,    {    'Content-Type':
'text/plain' });
  res.end('Hello, Kubernetes!');
};

const            server            =
http.createServer(requestListener);
server.listen(8080, () => {
```

170

```
console.log('Server is running on port
8080');
});
```

2. **Create a Dockerfile**: Next, create a `Dockerfile` to containerize the application:

```
Dockerfile

# Use the official Node.js image from the
Docker Hub
FROM node:14

# Set the working directory
WORKDIR /usr/src/app

#  package.json and install dependencies
 package*.json ./
RUN npm install

#  the application code
 . .

# Expose port 8080
EXPOSE 8080

# Command to run the application
CMD [ "node", "app.js" ]
```

3. **Build the Docker Image**: Run the following command in your terminal to build the Docker image:

```bash
bash
```

```bash
docker build -t my-node-app .
```

4. **Run the Docker Container Locally**: Test the Docker container locally:

```bash
bash
```

```bash
docker run -p 8080:8080 my-node-app
```

You should be able to access the application at http://localhost:8080.

Step 2: Push the Docker Image to a Container Registry

1. **Tag the Docker Image**: Tag the Docker image with the appropriate registry:

```bash
bash
```

```bash
docker tag my-node-app:latest <your-dockerhub-username>/my-node-app:latest
```

2. **Login to Docker Hub**: Log in to Docker Hub using your credentials:

```
bash
```

```
docker login
```

3. **Push the Image to Docker Hub**: Push the Docker image to Docker Hub:

```
bash
```

```
docker push <your-dockerhub-username>/my-
node-app:latest
```

Step 3: Create Kubernetes Configuration Files

1. **Create a Deployment Configuration (deployment.yaml)**: This configuration will define how Kubernetes should deploy your containerized application.

```
yaml
```

```yaml
apiVersion: apps/v1
kind: Deployment
metadata:
  name: my-node-app
spec:
  replicas: 3
  selector:
    matchLabels:
      app: my-node-app
  template:
```

```
metadata:
  labels:
    app: my-node-app
spec:
  containers:
  - name: my-node-app
    image:              <your-dockerhub-
username>/my-node-app:latest
    ports:
    - containerPort: 8080
```

In this file, we define a Kubernetes deployment that will run 3 replicas of our Node.js application.

2. **Create a Service Configuration (service.yaml)**: This configuration will expose the application to the outside world.

```
yaml

apiVersion: v1
kind: Service
metadata:
  name: my-node-app-service
spec:
  selector:
    app: my-node-app
  ports:
    - protocol: TCP
```

174

```
    port: 80
    targetPort: 8080
type: LoadBalancer
```

This service exposes the Node.js application on port 80 and forwards traffic to port 8080 inside the containers.

Step 4: Deploy the Application to Kubernetes

1. **Create a Kubernetes Cluster**: If you don't already have a Kubernetes cluster, you can set up one using **Google Kubernetes Engine (GKE)**, **Amazon EKS**, or **Azure AKS**. Alternatively, use **minikube** for local testing.

2. **Apply the Kubernetes Configuration**: Run the following commands to apply the deployment and service configurations to your Kubernetes cluster:

   bash

   ```
   kubectl apply -f deployment.yaml
   kubectl apply -f service.yaml
   ```

3. **Check the Deployment**: To verify that the application is running and pods have been created, use:

   bash

   ```
   kubectl get pods
   ```

4. **Access the Application**: If you're using a **LoadBalancer** type service, Kubernetes will provision an external IP for you. To find it, run:

```bash
bash
```

```
kubectl get svc
```

Access the application using the external IP.

Conclusion

In this chapter, we covered the basics of **containers** and **Docker**, explaining how they provide a lightweight and consistent way to deploy applications. We also discussed **Kubernetes** and its role in orchestrating containers, managing scaling, deployment, and ensuring high availability. By working through an example of deploying a **Node.js** application in Kubernetes, we demonstrated how containers and Kubernetes can work together to simplify application deployment and management.

Serverless computing and containers are powerful tools, but Kubernetes takes container management to the next level by providing sophisticated orchestration and scaling capabilities. By incorporating Kubernetes into your cloud-native architecture, you can efficiently manage containerized applications and scale them as needed.

CHAPTER 17

CLOUD-BASED CI/CD PIPELINES

In the fast-paced world of software development, **Continuous Integration (CI)** and **Continuous Deployment (CD)** have become essential practices for delivering software quickly and reliably. CI/CD pipelines automate the process of building, testing, and deploying applications, allowing teams to focus on writing code while ensuring quality and consistency. In this chapter, we will explore how CI/CD works in the cloud, how to set up a CI/CD pipeline using cloud-native tools, and provide an example using **Azure DevOps**.

How Continuous Integration and Continuous Deployment Work in the Cloud

1. What is Continuous Integration (CI)?

Continuous Integration is a development practice where developers regularly merge their code changes into a shared repository. Each integration is verified by an automated build and automated tests, ensuring that errors are caught early in the development process.

How CI works:

- **Version Control**: Developers commit code to a version control system (e.g., Git).
- **Automated Build**: Once code is committed, an automated build system compiles the code, installs dependencies, and packages the application.
- **Automated Testing**: After the build, automated tests are run (unit tests, integration tests) to verify that the code behaves as expected.
- **Feedback**: If any step fails (build or tests), the team is notified so they can fix issues quickly.

Benefits of CI:

- **Early Detection of Bugs**: CI helps identify bugs and issues early in the development cycle, reducing the risk of major issues during later stages.
- **Improved Collaboration**: By continuously integrating code, teams can work together more effectively and avoid integration problems.
- **Faster Development**: CI reduces the time needed for manual testing, enabling faster iterations and development cycles.

2. What is Continuous Deployment (CD)?

Continuous Deployment automates the release of applications into production. With CD, every change that passes the CI pipeline is automatically deployed to a production environment without manual intervention.

How CD works:

- **Automated Deployment**: After passing CI, the application is automatically deployed to the production environment.
- **Environment Configuration**: CD systems manage configuration changes, ensuring that environments are consistent and that new code doesn't break existing features.
- **Monitoring and Rollback**: If something goes wrong in production, CD tools can roll back to a previous version, ensuring high availability and reliability.

Benefits of CD:

- **Faster Time to Market**: CD enables rapid delivery of new features and fixes to production, improving the responsiveness of the team to customer needs.
- **Consistency Across Environments**: CD ensures that the same application is deployed in every environment (development, staging, production), reducing configuration drift and inconsistencies.

- **Minimized Risk**: Frequent, small releases reduce the risk of major failures in production since each deployment is a small change.

3. How CI/CD Works in the Cloud

In a cloud-based environment, CI/CD pipelines are typically hosted on cloud platforms, taking advantage of cloud-native tools and services for automation, scalability, and security. Cloud providers offer services like **AWS CodePipeline**, **Azure DevOps**, and **Google Cloud Build** to support CI/CD workflows.

Key Benefits of Cloud-based CI/CD:

- **Scalability**: Cloud infrastructure can scale automatically based on demand, allowing for efficient resource utilization during build, test, and deployment stages.
- **Integration with Cloud Services**: Cloud-based CI/CD pipelines can easily integrate with other cloud services like databases, storage, and monitoring tools, ensuring that all parts of the application are tested and deployed seamlessly.
- **Cost Efficiency**: Cloud providers typically offer pay-as-you-go pricing for CI/CD tools, allowing you to only pay for the resources you use during build and deployment.

Setting Up a CI/CD Pipeline Using Cloud-Native Tools

There are several cloud-native tools available for setting up CI/CD pipelines. In this section, we will walk through the steps of setting up a CI/CD pipeline using **Azure DevOps**, which is a comprehensive tool for CI/CD that integrates with other Azure services.

1. Setting Up Azure DevOps

Azure DevOps provides a suite of development tools for planning, building, testing, and deploying applications. It includes services for **Azure Pipelines, Azure Repos, Azure Artifacts**, and **Azure Test Plans**.

To get started with **Azure DevOps**, follow these steps:

1. **Sign Up for Azure DevOps**: Go to Azure DevOps and sign up for a free account or use an existing Microsoft account.
2. **Create a New Project**:
   o After logging in, click **Create Project** to start a new DevOps project.
   o Name your project and select visibility (Private or Public).
3. **Set Up Repositories**:

o Azure DevOps allows you to host code repositories using **Azure Repos**. You can either import an existing Git repository or create a new repository to store your application code.

o For this example, let's assume you have a Node.js application stored in a Git repository.

2. Create a Build Pipeline

A **build pipeline** automates the process of building and testing your application. In Azure DevOps, this is done using **Azure Pipelines**.

1. **Navigate to Pipelines**: In the Azure DevOps portal, go to the **Pipelines** section and click on **New Pipeline**.

2. **Select Your Repository**: Choose the repository that contains your application code (e.g., Azure Repos or GitHub).

3. **Define Build Steps**:
   o Select the type of pipeline (e.g., **YAML pipeline** for more flexibility or **Classic Editor** for a GUI-based approach).
   o In the YAML file, define the steps for building your application. For example:

```
yaml
```

```
trigger:
  branches:
    include:
      - main

pool:
  vmImage: 'ubuntu-latest'

steps:
- task: UseNode@1
  inputs:
    versionSpec: '14.x'
    addToPath: true

- script: |
    npm install
    npm run build
  displayName: 'Install dependencies and build'

- task: PublishBuildArtifacts@1
  inputs:
    publishLocation: 'Container'
    artifactName: 'drop'
```

   o This pipeline installs dependencies, runs the build, and publishes the build artifacts.

4. **Run the Build**:
After setting up the pipeline, save and run the build. The

pipeline will automatically trigger whenever there are changes in the repository (e.g., code commits).

3. Create a Release Pipeline

A **release pipeline** automates the deployment of the application to different environments (e.g., development, staging, production).

1. **Navigate   to   Releases**:
   In Azure DevOps, go to the **Releases** section and click **New Pipeline**.
2. **Define Stages**:
   - o Create multiple stages for different environments (e.g., **Dev**, **Test**, **Prod**).
   - o For each stage, define the deployment steps, such as deploying to Azure Web App or Azure Kubernetes Service (AKS).
3. **Link the Build Pipeline**:
   - o In the release pipeline, link the previously defined build pipeline. This will trigger the deployment process once the build is completed successfully.
4. **Deploy the Application**:
   - o In each stage, define the necessary deployment steps:
       - ▪ For example, if you are deploying to **Azure Web App**, use the **Azure App**

185

> **Service Deploy** task to deploy the build artifact.
>
> - If deploying to **Kubernetes**, use the **kubectl** task to apply the Kubernetes YAML files.

5. **Configure Approvals**:
   o Set up manual or automatic approvals before deploying to sensitive environments like production.
   o You can define conditions and requirements for each environment.

6. **Run the Release**:
   Trigger the release pipeline, and your application will be deployed automatically to the specified environments based on the pipeline configuration.

Example: Setting Up a CI/CD Pipeline with Azure DevOps

Let's consider a simple example of a Node.js web application. You want to automate the following steps:

1. **Build the application** using **npm**.
2. **Test the application** using **unit tests**.
3. **Deploy the application** to **Azure Web Apps**.

Here's how you can set up the CI/CD pipeline in Azure DevOps:

Step 1: Set Up the Build Pipeline (CI)

1. In the **Pipelines** section of Azure DevOps, create a new pipeline.
2. Select your **Git repository**.
3. Define the YAML for the build pipeline:

```yaml
yaml

trigger:
  branches:
    include:
      - main

pool:
  vmImage: 'ubuntu-latest'

steps:
- task: UseNode@1
  inputs:
    versionSpec: '14.x'
    addToPath: true

- script: |
    npm install
    npm test
```

```
displayName: 'Install dependencies and
run tests'

- task: PublishBuildArtifacts@1
  inputs:
    publishLocation: 'Container'
    artifactName: 'drop'
```

4. Save and run the build pipeline.

Step 2: Set Up the Release Pipeline (CD)

1. In the **Releases** section, create a new release pipeline.
2. Add the build artifact (from the build pipeline) as the source.
3. Define the deployment stages for each environment (e.g., **Dev, Staging, Production**).
4. For each environment, add the **Azure Web App Deploy** task:

```yaml
yaml

- task: AzureWebApp@1
  inputs:
    azureSubscription:    '<Your    Azure
Subscription>'
    appName: '<Your App Name>'
```

```
package:
'$(System.DefaultWorkingDirectory)/drop/*
'
```

5. Trigger the release and automatically deploy your app to Azure.

Conclusion

In this chapter, we introduced the concept of **Continuous Integration (CI)** and **Continuous Deployment (CD)**, focusing on their role in automating the process of building, testing, and deploying applications. We discussed how CI/CD works in the cloud and explored cloud-native tools for building CI/CD pipelines. Using **Azure DevOps**, we walked through the process of setting up a complete CI/CD pipeline that automates the build and deployment of a Node.js application. By implementing CI/CD pipelines, you can streamline your development workflow, reduce errors, and ensure that applications are quickly and consistently delivered to production.

CHAPTER 18

CLOUD AI AND MACHINE LEARNING SERVICES

Cloud platforms have made **Artificial Intelligence (AI)** and **Machine Learning (ML)** more accessible, enabling businesses and developers to build intelligent applications without needing specialized hardware or deep expertise in data science. In this chapter, we will explore the **AI and ML tools in the cloud**, how to implement AI/ML using cloud services, and provide a hands-on example of using **AWS SageMaker** to build a machine learning model.

Overview of AI and Machine Learning Tools in the Cloud

Cloud providers offer a range of AI and machine learning tools that can help organizations and developers easily integrate advanced algorithms and capabilities into their applications. These services handle the complexity of training models, optimizing performance, and managing infrastructure. Here is a look at the main AI/ML services offered by the major cloud providers.

1. Amazon Web Services (AWS)

AWS offers a comprehensive suite of AI and ML tools that cater to different stages of machine learning workflows. Key services include:

- **Amazon SageMaker**: A fully managed service that allows developers and data scientists to quickly build, train, and deploy machine learning models. SageMaker offers built-in algorithms, model training, and deployment solutions, and it supports various machine learning frameworks (e.g., TensorFlow, PyTorch).

- **AWS Deep Learning AMIs**: Amazon Machine Images that come pre-configured with deep learning frameworks and tools to support building custom ML models.

- **Amazon Rekognition**: A service for image and video analysis, such as object recognition, facial analysis, and text recognition.

- **Amazon Polly**: A service that converts text to lifelike speech, enabling voice-based applications.

- **Amazon Lex**: A service to build conversational interfaces using voice or text, powered by the same deep learning technologies used by Alexa.

2. Microsoft Azure

Azure provides a wide array of machine learning and AI services tailored to both developers and data scientists. Key services include:

- **Azure Machine Learning**: A comprehensive, cloud-based data science platform that helps developers build, train, and deploy models using tools such as Jupyter notebooks and automated machine learning (AutoML).

- **Azure Cognitive Services**: A set of pre-built AI APIs that provide functionality for vision (e.g., face recognition, image analysis), language (e.g., text analytics, language translation), and speech (e.g., speech recognition and synthesis).

- **Azure Bot Services**: A platform for building, testing, and deploying intelligent bots that can engage with users through chat, voice, and other channels.

3. Google Cloud Platform (GCP)

Google Cloud also offers robust AI and ML tools, with services that leverage Google's deep expertise in AI. Key services include:

- **Google AI Platform**: A unified environment for building, training, and deploying machine learning models. It supports popular ML frameworks (TensorFlow, PyTorch, scikit-learn) and provides tools for both data scientists and developers.

- **AutoML**: A suite of machine learning tools that automatically build custom models based on your data, even if you don't have an extensive machine learning background.

- **Google Vision AI**: A suite of tools for image analysis, including object detection, label detection, and optical character recognition (OCR).

- **Dialogflow**: A platform for building conversational interfaces, including chatbots and virtual assistants.

How to Implement AI/ML Using Cloud Services

Implementing AI and machine learning models in the cloud can significantly reduce the time and resources required to build intelligent applications. Here are the key steps involved in using cloud services for AI/ML:

1. Data Collection and Preparation

The first step in any machine learning workflow is to collect and prepare data. Cloud services provide several options for storing and preparing data, including:

- **Cloud Storage**: Services like **Amazon S3, Azure Blob Storage**, and **Google Cloud Storage** allow you to store large datasets for training machine learning models.
- **Data Preparation Tools**: Tools like **AWS Glue, Azure Data Factory**, and **Google Cloud Dataprep** allow you to transform, clean, and preprocess data before feeding it into machine learning models.

2. Model Building

Once the data is prepared, the next step is to build the machine learning model. Cloud providers offer tools and services to help you create, train, and test models efficiently:

- **Pre-built Algorithms**: Services like **AWS SageMaker, Azure Machine Learning**, and **Google AI Platform** offer pre-built algorithms for common tasks such as regression, classification, and clustering.
- **Custom Models**: If you have more specific needs, cloud services support custom model development using popular frameworks like **TensorFlow, PyTorch**, and **scikit-learn**.

3. Model Training

Training a machine learning model typically requires significant computational resources. Cloud services provide the ability to scale training jobs with GPU or TPU instances:

- **AWS SageMaker** offers managed training environments with scalable infrastructure and automatic model tuning.
- **Azure Machine Learning** provides a distributed training environment with built-in experiment tracking and versioning.
- **Google AI Platform** offers training on both CPUs and GPUs, and you can use **Google Cloud's TPUs** for even faster training on deep learning models.

4. Model Deployment

After training a model, it needs to be deployed for use in production. Cloud services provide several ways to deploy machine learning models:

- **Real-time Inference**: Services like **AWS Lambda**, **Azure Functions**, and **Google Cloud Functions** can run trained models in real-time for applications like predictions or classifications.
- **Batch Inference**: For non-real-time use cases, batch processing tools like **AWS Batch** and **Google Cloud Dataflow** allow you to run predictions on large datasets in parallel.

5. Model Monitoring and Maintenance

Once a model is deployed, it is important to monitor its performance and retrain it if necessary. Cloud services offer tools to monitor models and data pipelines, and you can set up automated retraining based on new data.

- **AWS SageMaker** offers model monitoring to track drift in predictions and trigger retraining when necessary.
- **Azure Machine Learning** provides logging and performance tracking for deployed models.

Example: Using AWS SageMaker to Build a Machine Learning Model

Let's walk through an example of using **AWS SageMaker** to build and deploy a machine learning model for predicting housing prices based on various features (e.g., location, number of bedrooms, square footage).

Step 1: Set Up AWS SageMaker

1. **Create an AWS Account**: Sign up for an AWS account at AWS.
2. **Access SageMaker**: In the AWS Management Console, search for **SageMaker** and click on it to access the SageMaker dashboard.
3. **Create a New Notebook Instance**:

- o In SageMaker, create a new notebook instance to write and run your code.
- o Choose an instance type (e.g., `ml.t2.medium` for small workloads).

Step 2: Load and Prepare the Data

1. **Upload Data to Amazon S3**:
   - o Upload your dataset (e.g., CSV file with housing data) to an **Amazon S3 bucket**.
   - o You can do this via the S3 dashboard in the AWS Management Console or using the AWS CLI.

2. **Data Preprocessing**:
   - o Open your SageMaker notebook instance and import the necessary libraries:

   python

   ```
   import boto3
   import pandas as pd
   import sagemaker
   from         sagemaker        import
   get_execution_role
   from sklearn.model_selection import
   train_test_split
   ```

   - o Load the data from S3:

   python

```
s3 = boto3.client('s3')
data    =    pd.read_csv('s3://<your-
bucket-name>/housing_data.csv')
```

o Preprocess the data (e.g., handling missing values, encoding categorical features, scaling numerical features).

Step 3: Train the Model

1. **Choose an Algorithm**:
   o AWS SageMaker offers several built-in algorithms for common ML tasks. For this example, we'll use the **XGBoost** algorithm, which is suitable for regression tasks like predicting housing prices.
2. **Set Up the Training Job**:
   o Define the training job and specify the location of the dataset in S3:

```python
from    sagemaker.sklearn    import
SKLearnModel

# Define the model and train
xgboost_model                    =
sagemaker.estimator.Estimator(
```

```
image_uri=sagemaker.image_uris.retr
ieve('xgboost',
region=boto3.Session().region_name,
version='1.0-1'),
    role=get_execution_role(),
    instance_count=1,
    instance_type='ml.m4.xlarge',
)
xgboost_model.fit({'train':
's3://<your-bucket-
name>/housing_train.csv'})
```

Step 4: Deploy the Model

1. **Deploy the Trained Model**:
   o After training the model, deploy it to an endpoint for real-time inference:

   ```python
   python
   ```

   ```python
   predictor = xgboost_model.deploy(
       initial_instance_count=1,
       instance_type='ml.m4.xlarge'
   )
   ```

2. **Invoke the Model Endpoint**:
   o Once the model is deployed, you can send new data to the endpoint for predictions:

199

```python
python

predictions                              =
predictor.predict(new_data)
print(predictions)
```

Step 5: Monitor and Maintain the Model

1. **Monitor Performance**:
   o Use SageMaker Model Monitor to track changes in prediction quality and detect model drift.
   o If the model's performance decreases, retrain the model with new data.

Conclusion

In this chapter, we introduced **cloud-based AI and machine learning services**, focusing on the tools offered by **AWS**, **Azure**, and **Google Cloud**. We explored how to implement AI and ML using cloud services, from data preparation to model deployment. The example using **AWS SageMaker** demonstrated how easy it is to build, train, and deploy a machine learning model using a fully managed service. With cloud-based AI/ML services, businesses and developers can leverage advanced capabilities without needing deep expertise in infrastructure management, making AI and machine learning more accessible and cost-effective.

CHAPTER 19

CLOUD MIGRATION STRATEGIES

As businesses move to the cloud, migrating existing applications from on-premise infrastructure to the cloud has become a critical task. The process of **cloud migration** involves transferring applications, data, and services from traditional environments to cloud-based platforms like **AWS**, **Azure**, or **Google Cloud**. This chapter explores the different strategies for cloud migration, tools and best practices to ensure a smooth transition, and provides a hands-on example of migrating a **WordPress** site to **AWS**.

Moving Existing Applications to the Cloud

1. Why Migrate to the Cloud?

Cloud migration offers a range of benefits, including:

- **Cost Efficiency**: Moving to the cloud can reduce capital expenditures for hardware and infrastructure, shifting costs to a more flexible operational expense model.
- **Scalability**: Cloud environments automatically scale based on demand, ensuring that applications can handle spikes in traffic or data without manual intervention.

- **Disaster Recovery and Backup**: Cloud platforms provide built-in disaster recovery options and automated backups to protect against data loss.
- **Flexibility and Agility**: Cloud infrastructure allows organizations to innovate faster, as they can quickly provision new services or resources without waiting for physical hardware.

2. Types of Cloud Migration

There are several approaches to cloud migration, each suited to different needs and scenarios. The most common migration strategies are:

1. Rehosting ("Lift and Shift")

- **What it is**: Rehosting involves moving an application to the cloud with minimal changes to the application or its infrastructure. Essentially, you replicate the application in the cloud, maintaining the current architecture and setup.
- **When to use**: This strategy is often used when businesses need to move quickly to the cloud without making significant changes to the application.
- **Benefits**: Quick to implement, minimal upfront investment.

- **Challenges**: Doesn't take full advantage of cloud-native features and may not optimize performance or costs in the long term.

2. Replatforming ("Lift, Tinker, and Shift")

- **What it is**: Replatforming involves making some optimizations to the application while migrating it to the cloud. This might include changing the database engine or updating the app to work better in the cloud, but the overall architecture remains the same.
- **When to use**: Suitable when some changes are needed to improve performance or scalability but a full rewrite is unnecessary.
- **Benefits**: Faster than a complete refactor while still improving the app's performance and scalability in the cloud.
- **Challenges**: Requires more effort than a "lift and shift" migration.

3. Refactoring (Re-architecting)

- **What it is**: Refactoring involves completely redesigning and rebuilding the application to take full advantage of cloud-native features such as microservices, containerization, or serverless computing.

- **When to use**: Suitable when an application is outdated or inefficient, and a major overhaul is needed to modernize it for the cloud.
- **Benefits**: Leverages the full benefits of cloud-native architectures (e.g., scalability, cost optimization, flexibility).
- **Challenges**: Time-consuming, expensive, and requires significant expertise.

4. Retiring

- **What it is**: Retiring involves removing applications that are no longer needed or replacing them with cloud-native solutions.
- **When to use**: This approach is used when certain applications or services are no longer useful or have become obsolete.
- **Benefits**: Reduces complexity and cloud costs.
- **Challenges**: Requires careful planning to ensure business continuity and minimize disruptions.

5. Retaining

- **What it is**: In some cases, businesses may choose to keep certain applications on-premises due to regulatory, compliance, or technical reasons. This strategy is known as "retaining."

- **When to use**: When there are technical, security, or compliance reasons to keep an application on-premises while the rest of the infrastructure is moved to the cloud.
- **Benefits**: Ensures that critical systems remain secure and compliant.
- **Challenges**: May lead to hybrid environments, adding complexity to operations.

Tools and Best Practices for Cloud Migration

1. Cloud Migration Tools

Cloud providers offer various tools to assist with migration, automating much of the process and reducing risks.

- **AWS Migration Tools**:
    - **AWS Migration Hub**: Provides a central location to track the progress of application migrations across AWS services.
    - **AWS Server Migration Service (SMS)**: A service that automates the migration of on-premise servers to AWS.
    - **AWS Database Migration Service (DMS)**: Helps migrate databases to AWS with minimal downtime.

- o **AWS Application Discovery Service**: Helps identify application dependencies, making it easier to plan the migration.
- **Azure Migration Tools**:
  - o **Azure Migrate**: A centralized hub for all Azure migration tools, helping with discovery, assessment, and migration of workloads to Azure.
  - o **Azure Site Recovery**: Provides replication and disaster recovery capabilities to help move applications to Azure with minimal downtime.
  - o **Azure Database Migration Service**: Simplifies the process of migrating databases to Azure.
- **Google Cloud Migration Tools**:
  - o **Google Cloud Migrate for Compute Engine**: A tool for moving virtual machines from on-premise or other cloud environments to Google Cloud.
  - o **Database Migration Service**: Helps migrate databases to Google Cloud with minimal downtime.

2. Best Practices for Cloud Migration

- **Plan and Assess**:
  - o Perform a detailed **cost analysis** to estimate cloud expenses and compare them to on-premises costs.

- o **Audit** your existing infrastructure to determine which applications can be moved, refactored, or retired.
- o **Prioritize** applications based on business needs, complexity, and readiness for cloud migration.

- **Test Before Full Migration**:
  - o Run **pilot migrations** for a subset of applications to identify any challenges before migrating the entire infrastructure.
  - o Use cloud migration tools to simulate and test the migration process.

- **Monitor and Optimize Post-Migration**:
  - o After migrating applications to the cloud, **monitor** their performance and costs closely to ensure they are running optimally.
  - o Use **cloud-native monitoring tools** (e.g., **AWS CloudWatch**, **Azure Monitor**, **Google Cloud Operations Suite**) to track performance, errors, and resource usage.

- **Ensure Security and Compliance**:
  - o Ensure that **security measures** (e.g., encryption, identity management, access controls) are in place during the migration process.
  - o Understand the **compliance requirements** for your industry and ensure that the cloud provider's solutions meet those standards.

Example: Migrating a WordPress Site to AWS

Let's walk through an example of migrating a **WordPress** site to **AWS**. This will involve setting up the necessary AWS services, migrating the WordPress files and database, and ensuring that the site works in the cloud.

Step 1: Set Up AWS Infrastructure

1. **Create an EC2 Instance**:
   o Log into the **AWS Management Console** and navigate to **EC2**.
   o Launch an **EC2 instance** using the **Amazon Linux 2** or **Ubuntu** AMI.
   o Choose an instance type (e.g., **t2.micro** for small-scale websites).
   o Configure the instance with appropriate security groups (e.g., allowing HTTP/HTTPS traffic on ports 80 and 443).

2. **Install LAMP Stack** (Linux, Apache, MySQL, PHP):
   o SSH into your EC2 instance and install the required software:

```bash

sudo yum update -y
```

208

```
sudo yum install -y httpd mariadb-server
php php-mysqlnd php-fpm
```

- o   Start the Apache and MySQL services:

```
bash
```

```
sudo service httpd start
sudo service mariadb start
```

- o   Enable them to start on boot:

```
bash
```

```
sudo systemctl enable httpd
sudo systemctl enable mariadb
```

Step 2: Move WordPress Files and Database

1. **Export WordPress Files**:
   - o   On your existing WordPress site, use **FTP** or **cPanel** to download all WordPress files from your current server, including the wp-content directory and wp-config.php file.
2. **Import WordPress Files to EC2**:
   - o   Upload the downloaded files to your EC2 instance's web root (e.g., /var/www/html):

```
bash
```

```
scp   -r   /path/to/wordpress/*   ec2-
user@<EC2_IP>:/var/www/html/
```

3. **Export and Import the Database**:
   - o Export the WordPress database from your existing server using **phpMyAdmin** or the `mysqldump` command:

```
bash
```

```
mysqldump -u <username> -p <database_name>
> wordpress_backup.sql
```

   - o Import the database into your new MySQL server on EC2:

```
bash
```

```
mysql -u root -p <wordpress_backup.sql
```

4. **Update the Database Configuration**:
   - o Edit the `wp-config.php` file to match your new database settings (e.g., database name, username, password, and host).

Step 3: Configure Domain and SSL

1. **Update DNS Settings**:

o   Point your domain's **A record** to the public IP address of your EC2 instance.

2. **Install SSL** (optional but recommended):

o   Install **Let's Encrypt SSL** using the `certbot` tool:

```bash
sudo yum install -y certbot python2-certbot-apache
sudo certbot --apache
```

Step 4: Test the WordPress Site

Once the migration is complete, navigate to your domain in a web browser to ensure that the WordPress site is fully functional. Verify that the pages load correctly, images are displayed, and the database is connected properly.

Conclusion

In this chapter, we covered **cloud migration strategies**, including **rehosting, replatforming, refactoring, retiring,** and **retaining**. We explored the tools and best practices for cloud migration, emphasizing the importance of proper planning, testing, and optimization. The example of migrating a **WordPress** site to **AWS** demonstrated a typical cloud migration process, from setting up an EC2 instance and installing a LAMP stack to transferring files and databases.

Cloud migration is a complex but essential process, and choosing the right strategy and tools can ensure a smooth transition to the cloud. By leveraging cloud-native services and adhering to best practices, businesses can successfully modernize their infrastructure, improve performance, and reduce costs.

CHAPTER 20

CLOUD APPLICATION DEVELOPMENT FRAMEWORKS

Cloud computing has transformed how applications are developed, deployed, and managed. Cloud application development frameworks provide developers with the tools and libraries they need to build scalable, secure, and high-performing applications. These frameworks simplify common tasks like provisioning resources, managing authentication, and scaling applications, making it easier to build cloud-native applications. In this chapter, we will explore popular frameworks for cloud application development, discuss how to choose the right framework for your cloud application, and provide an example using the **Serverless Framework** to deploy an app.

Popular Frameworks for Cloud Application Development

Several cloud application development frameworks cater to different cloud platforms, architectures, and use cases. Here are some popular frameworks that simplify the process of developing and deploying cloud applications.

1. AWS Serverless Application Model (AWS SAM)

What **it** **is**:
AWS Serverless Application Model (AWS SAM) is a framework for building serverless applications on AWS. It simplifies the development, testing, and deployment of serverless applications using **AWS Lambda**, **API Gateway**, **DynamoDB**, and other AWS services.

Features:

- **Simplified Configuration**: SAM provides an easy-to-use syntax to define serverless resources, reducing the complexity of AWS CloudFormation templates.
- **Local Development**: SAM CLI allows you to locally test AWS Lambda functions and API Gateway endpoints before deploying them to AWS.
- **Deployment**: SAM integrates with AWS CloudFormation, enabling one-click deployments of serverless applications to the cloud.

Use Cases:

- Building serverless web apps.
- Creating REST APIs with Lambda functions.
- Real-time data processing applications.

2. Serverless Framework

What it is:
The **Serverless Framework** is a popular open-source framework for building serverless applications. It abstracts away the underlying infrastructure and makes it easier to develop, deploy, and monitor serverless applications across multiple cloud providers like AWS, Microsoft Azure, and Google Cloud Platform.

Features:

- **Multi-cloud Support**: While it is primarily used with AWS, the Serverless Framework also supports Azure, Google Cloud, and other cloud providers.
- **Zero Server Management**: Developers define functions, events, and resources in a configuration file, and the framework handles the provisioning and scaling.
- **Extensibility**: The Serverless Framework offers plugins to extend its functionality, such as integrations with monitoring tools, databases, and CI/CD pipelines.

Use Cases:

- Building microservices architectures.
- Developing event-driven applications.
- Creating APIs, CRON jobs, and data pipelines.

3. Spring Boot (for Java-based Cloud Apps)

What **it** **is**:
Spring Boot is an open-source framework for building Java-based applications that run in the cloud. It simplifies the development of production-ready applications with embedded servers and various tools for microservices architectures, security, and data access.

Features:

- **Rapid Development**: Spring Boot allows developers to create applications quickly with minimal configuration.
- **Microservices Support**: It integrates well with other Spring Cloud components, making it ideal for building microservices-based applications.
- **Cloud-Native**: Spring Boot supports cloud-based deployment options like **Cloud Foundry, AWS Elastic Beanstalk**, and **Kubernetes**.

Use Cases:

- Building cloud-native Java applications.
- Developing microservices architectures.
- Creating enterprise applications that require robust security and data access.

4. Django (for Python-based Cloud Apps)

What it is:
Django is a high-level Python web framework that enables rapid development of secure and scalable applications. Django is often used in cloud-based environments due to its simplicity and built-in tools for building database-backed web applications.

Features:

- **Built-in Authentication**: Django comes with pre-built authentication, authorization, and session management tools.
- **Rapid Prototyping**: Django's "batteries-included" philosophy allows developers to quickly prototype and develop applications with minimal configuration.
- **Scalability**: Django applications can scale easily on cloud platforms like AWS, Google Cloud, and Azure.

Use Cases:

- Building web applications, especially with heavy database interactions.
- Developing RESTful APIs using Django REST Framework.
- Cloud-based social media platforms, blogs, or e-commerce sites.

5. Flask (for Lightweight Python Apps)

What **it** **is**:
Flask is a micro-framework for Python that provides the core tools needed to build a web application. Flask is minimalistic, meaning developers can extend it as needed with various libraries and components, making it ideal for cloud-based apps where customizability is important.

Features:

- **Simplicity**: Flask provides a small core framework, leaving the decision of which libraries to use up to the developer.
- **Flexibility**: Flask is ideal for small to medium-sized applications and allows for easy integration with cloud platforms like AWS Lambda or Google Cloud Functions.
- **Modular**: Developers can add functionality incrementally by including external libraries.

Use Cases:

- Building lightweight cloud applications.
- Developing APIs for web and mobile applications.
- Serverless applications using AWS Lambda or Google Cloud Functions.

218

6. Firebase (for Real-time Cloud Apps)

What it is:
Firebase is a platform for building mobile and web applications, providing real-time databases, user authentication, hosting, and other backend services. It is particularly useful for developing cloud-native apps that require real-time capabilities, like chat applications or collaborative tools.

Features:

- **Real-time Database**: Firebase provides a NoSQL cloud database with real-time synchronization across clients.
- **Authentication**: Firebase offers pre-built authentication modules for easy user login with various providers (e.g., Google, Facebook, email).
- **Hosting and Serverless Functions**: Firebase supports serverless functions (via **Cloud Functions**) and hosting to serve dynamic content.

Use Cases:

- Real-time applications like chat or collaboration tools.
- Mobile-first cloud applications.
- Building scalable serverless apps with minimal configuration.

How to Choose the Right Framework for Your Cloud App

When choosing a framework for cloud application development, several factors should guide your decision-making process. Here are some things to consider:

1. Cloud Provider

- If you're committed to a specific cloud provider (e.g., AWS, Azure, Google Cloud), choosing a framework that integrates seamlessly with that platform can simplify deployment and management. For instance, **AWS SAM** or **Serverless Framework** works great with AWS, while **Azure DevOps** and **Azure Functions** integrate well with Microsoft Azure.

2. Application Type

- If your application is a simple, stateless function (e.g., a REST API or data processing service), **Serverless Framework** or **AWS Lambda** is ideal.
- For large, enterprise-level applications requiring robust features like authentication, relational databases, and user management, **Spring Boot** or **Django** may be more appropriate.

- If real-time communication or mobile backend services are needed, **Firebase** is a strong choice.

3. Scalability and Flexibility

- If scalability is a priority, **Kubernetes** (with frameworks like **Spring Cloud** or **Django**) can help you manage containerized applications at scale. Alternatively, serverless options like the **Serverless Framework** or **AWS Lambda** offer automatic scaling without manual intervention.

4. Development Speed and Complexity

- For rapid development, **Django** and **Flask** provide excellent frameworks that reduce boilerplate code, whereas **Serverless Framework** allows you to rapidly build and deploy event-driven applications with minimal configuration.
- For a simpler, lightweight approach, **Flask** or **Firebase** might be better for smaller apps or MVPs (Minimum Viable Products).

5. Ecosystem and Community Support

- Consider the maturity of the framework and the level of community support available. Frameworks like **Spring Boot** and **Django** have large communities and extensive documentation, while **Serverless Framework** is well-supported for cloud-native applications.

Example: Using the Serverless Framework to Deploy an App

The **Serverless Framework** simplifies the process of deploying serverless applications across multiple cloud providers. In this example, we will deploy a simple **Node.js** app using the **Serverless Framework** on AWS.

Step 1: Install Serverless Framework

1. First, install the Serverless Framework globally using npm:

```bash

npm install -g serverless
```

Step 2: Create a Serverless Project

1. Create a new service (project) by running:

```bash

serverless create --template aws-nodejs --path my-service
```

222

```
cd my-service
```

2. This will generate a basic Node.js project with a
    serverless configuration file (`serverless.yml`).

Step 3: Define the Serverless Function

In the `serverless.yml` file, define your function and its trigger:

yaml

```
service: my-service

provider:
  name: aws
  runtime: nodejs14.x

functions:
  hello:
    handler: handler.hello
    events:
      - http:
          path: hello
          method: get
```

This configuration sets up a Lambda function (`hello`) that is
triggered by HTTP GET requests to the `/hello` path.

Step 4: Write the Function Code

In the `handler.js` file, write the function that will be executed when the endpoint is hit:

javascript

```javascript
module.exports.hello = async (event) => {
  return {
    statusCode: 200,
    body: JSON.stringify({ message: 'Hello,
Serverless!' }),
  };
};
```

Step 5: Deploy the Application

1. Deploy the serverless function to AWS by running:

    bash

    ```bash
    serverless deploy
    ```

2. The Serverless Framework will package your function, create the necessary AWS resources (like Lambda, API Gateway), and deploy the application.

Step 6: Test the Deployed API

After deployment, the framework will output the API Gateway endpoint URL. Test the deployed application by visiting the URL in your browser:

```bash

https://<your-api-id>.execute-
api.<region>.amazonaws.com/dev/hello
```

You should see the message: `{"message":"Hello, Serverless!"}`.

Conclusion

In this chapter, we explored **cloud application development frameworks** and how they help streamline the development, deployment, and scaling of cloud-native applications. We reviewed popular frameworks such as **AWS SAM, Serverless Framework, Spring Boot, Django**, and **Firebase**, each catering to different types of cloud applications and development needs.

We also walked through a practical example of deploying a serverless app using the **Serverless Framework** on AWS. By leveraging cloud frameworks like these, developers can focus more on building application features and less on managing infrastructure, ultimately speeding up development and reducing operational overhead.

CHAPTER 21

CLOUD COMPLIANCE AND LEGAL CONSIDERATIONS

As businesses move to the cloud, ensuring compliance with various regulations and legal requirements becomes a critical part of the process. These regulations govern how sensitive data is handled, stored, and transmitted, and failure to comply can lead to legal repercussions, financial penalties, and reputational damage. This chapter will explore cloud compliance frameworks such as **GDPR** and **HIPAA**, how to ensure your cloud setup meets regulatory requirements, and provide a practical example of setting up **GDPR-compliant cloud services**.

Understanding Cloud Compliance Frameworks

Cloud compliance involves ensuring that your cloud applications and services meet the regulatory requirements and standards set by various laws, industry standards, and frameworks. The most common compliance frameworks for cloud applications include:

1. General Data Protection Regulation (GDPR)

What **it** **is**:
The **General Data Protection Regulation (GDPR)** is a

regulation established by the European Union (EU) to protect the personal data and privacy of EU citizens. GDPR applies to any organization that processes personal data of EU citizens, regardless of where the organization is located.

Key Requirements:

- **Data Subject Rights**: GDPR grants individuals several rights, including the right to access, correct, delete, and port their data.
- **Data Protection by Design and by Default**: Organizations must integrate privacy and data protection features into their systems from the outset.
- **Data Processing Agreements**: Cloud providers must ensure that they process data in compliance with GDPR, and organizations must have contracts in place (Data Processing Agreements, or DPAs) that govern the processing of data.

Penalties:

Organizations that fail to comply with GDPR can face fines of up to **€20 million** or **4% of annual global turnover**, whichever is higher.

2. Health Insurance Portability and Accountability Act (HIPAA)

What **it** **is**:

HIPAA is a U.S. law designed to protect the privacy and security of healthcare data, including **Protected Health Information (PHI)**. It applies to healthcare providers, insurers, and their partners who handle sensitive patient data.

Key Requirements:

- **Security Rule**: HIPAA mandates specific administrative, physical, and technical safeguards to ensure that PHI is protected from unauthorized access and breaches.
- **Privacy Rule**: HIPAA requires that healthcare organizations obtain patient consent before sharing PHI and ensures that patients have access to their own data.
- **Business Associate Agreements (BAAs)**: Organizations must sign a BAA with cloud providers to ensure that both parties are compliant with HIPAA when handling PHI.

Penalties:

Non-compliance with HIPAA can result in fines ranging from **$100 to $50,000** per violation, with a maximum penalty of **$1.5 million** per year.

3. Federal Risk and Authorization Management Program (FedRAMP)

What **it** **is**:

FedRAMP is a U.S. government program that provides a standardized approach to security assessment, authorization, and continuous monitoring for cloud products and services. It is required for cloud services used by U.S. federal agencies.

Key Requirements:

- **Security Controls**: FedRAMP sets specific security controls based on the NIST 800-53 framework.
- **Assessment and Authorization**: Cloud service providers must undergo a rigorous assessment to be authorized for use by federal agencies.

4. Payment Card Industry Data Security Standard (PCI DSS)

What   it   is: PCI DSS is a global standard for any organization that processes, stores, or transmits credit card information. It ensures that credit card data is protected from fraud and theft.

Key Requirements:

- **Encryption**: PCI DSS requires that cardholder data be encrypted both in transit and at rest.
- **Access Control**: Only authorized personnel should have access to payment card information.
- **Security Monitoring**: Continuous monitoring of systems that store, process, or transmit payment card data to detect security breaches.

How to Ensure Your Cloud Setup Meets Regulatory Requirements

Ensuring that your cloud infrastructure is compliant with relevant regulations requires a combination of tools, processes, and strategies. Here are the key steps to follow:

1. Understand the Regulatory Requirements

Before migrating to the cloud or using cloud services, it's essential to thoroughly understand the compliance requirements relevant to your industry or geographic location. For example:

- If you're handling **personal data of EU citizens**, you need to comply with **GDPR**.
- If you're working with **healthcare data**, you need to ensure compliance with **HIPAA**.
- For **payment processing**, PCI DSS compliance is required.

2. Choose the Right Cloud Provider

Ensure that the cloud provider you choose has the necessary certifications and tools to meet your compliance requirements. For example:

- **AWS**, **Azure**, and **Google Cloud** offer a range of compliance certifications, including GDPR, HIPAA, and PCI DSS.
- Cloud providers typically provide **compliance whitepapers**, documentation, and certifications that demonstrate their adherence to industry standards.

3. Implement Security Best Practices

Ensure that your cloud setup incorporates the security controls necessary to protect sensitive data and meet regulatory standards. These include:

- **Data Encryption**: Ensure data is encrypted both in transit and at rest. Most cloud providers offer encryption features, such as **AWS KMS** (Key Management Service) or **Azure Key Vault**.
- **Access Control**: Implement strong access control mechanisms using **IAM (Identity and Access Management)** services to restrict access to sensitive data and systems. Use **multi-factor authentication (MFA)** to secure user accounts.
- **Audit Logging and Monitoring**: Enable logging and continuous monitoring of cloud resources to track access to sensitive data. Services like **AWS CloudTrail** and **Azure Monitor** provide detailed logs for auditing.

4. Use Compliance-Specific Tools and Services

Many cloud providers offer specialized services and tools to help with compliance:

- **AWS Artifact**: A service that provides access to compliance reports and security documentation.
- **Azure Compliance Manager**: A tool that helps assess your compliance posture and provides actionable recommendations.
- **Google Cloud Compliance**: Provides resources to understand compliance with GDPR, HIPAA, PCI DSS, and other frameworks.

5. Create Data Processing Agreements (DPAs) and Business Associate Agreements (BAAs)

When working with third-party cloud providers, ensure that you have a **Data Processing Agreement (DPA)** or **Business Associate Agreement (BAA)** in place. These agreements legally bind the cloud provider to adhere to the same compliance standards you are subject to.

6. Conduct Regular Compliance Audits

Cloud environments are dynamic, so it's essential to conduct regular compliance audits to ensure that your cloud infrastructure remains compliant with regulatory requirements. Many cloud providers offer tools for automating compliance checks, such as:

- **AWS Config**: Continuously monitors AWS resources for compliance with your security and compliance rules.
- **Azure Policy**: Helps enforce compliance with organizational standards by applying policies to resources.

Example: Setting Up GDPR-Compliant Cloud Services

Let's walk through an example of setting up GDPR-compliant cloud services on **AWS**. We will focus on the key aspects of GDPR, such as data protection, transparency, and access controls.

Step 1: Choose an AWS Region with GDPR Compliance

GDPR mandates that personal data of EU citizens should be stored and processed in compliance with EU data protection laws. To ensure GDPR compliance, select an **AWS region** that complies with GDPR, such as the **EU (Ireland)** or **EU (Frankfurt)** regions.

Step 2: Enable Data Encryption

Encrypting data is a fundamental requirement of GDPR. AWS provides several ways to encrypt data both at rest and in transit:

1. **S3 Bucket Encryption**:
   - o Enable **server-side encryption** for Amazon S3 buckets that store personal data:

   bash

   ```
   aws s3api put-bucket-encryption --bucket
   <your-bucket-name>         --server-side-
   encryption-configuration
   '{"Rules":[{"ApplyServerSideEncryptionByD
   efault":{"SSEAlgorithm":"AES256"}}]}'
   ```

2. **EBS Volume Encryption**:
   - o Enable encryption when creating Amazon EBS volumes to protect data stored on disk.

Step 3: Implement Access Control

Access control is crucial for GDPR compliance, ensuring that only authorized users can access personal data.

1. **AWS Identity and Access Management (IAM)**: Set up granular **IAM policies** to limit access to sensitive data.

2. **Enable Multi-Factor Authentication (MFA)** for all accounts that access personal data to add an extra layer of security.

3. Use **AWS IAM Access Analyzer** to ensure that permissions are correctly set and resources are properly secured.

Step 4: Set Up Data Processing Agreements (DPA)

1. When using AWS to process personal data, ensure that you have a **Data Processing Agreement (DPA)** in place. You can find AWS's DPA in the **AWS Artifact** service, where you can download and review the necessary legal agreements.

Step 5: Enable Logging and Monitoring

1. **Enable AWS CloudTrail** to log all API calls related to personal data. CloudTrail provides an audit trail of who accessed what data and when.

2. Use **Amazon CloudWatch** to monitor for unusual activity and potential security incidents, such as unauthorized access to sensitive data.

Step 6: Ensure Data Subject Rights

GDPR gives EU citizens the right to access, rectify, or delete their personal data. You need to implement processes for handling data subject requests:

1. Use **AWS Lambda** to automate the process of responding to requests to delete personal data stored in S3, databases, or other services.
2. Implement a **workflow** for verifying the identity of data subjects before granting access to their data.

Conclusion

In this chapter, we explored **cloud compliance frameworks** such as **GDPR, HIPAA**, and others, and discussed how to ensure your cloud setup meets these regulatory requirements. We reviewed tools and best practices for cloud compliance, such as data encryption, access control, logging, and audit trails. Finally, we walked through a practical example of setting up **GDPR-compliant services** on **AWS**, covering the essential steps needed to protect personal data and ensure compliance.

By understanding and implementing these cloud compliance frameworks and tools, businesses can protect sensitive data, avoid legal risks, and build trust with their customers. Compliance is an ongoing process, and regular audits and updates are necessary to keep up with evolving regulations and best practices.

CHAPTER 22

CLOUD DISASTER RECOVERY AND BACKUP SOLUTIONS

Disaster recovery (DR) and data backup are critical components of any organization's IT strategy, ensuring that data is protected and can be quickly restored in the event of a failure or disaster. Cloud services offer powerful tools for setting up disaster recovery and backup solutions that can enhance business continuity, reduce downtime, and minimize data loss. In this chapter, we will discuss how cloud services help with disaster recovery, how to set up automated backups and failover strategies, and provide an example of setting up a backup solution in **AWS using Glacier**.

How Cloud Services Help with Disaster Recovery

Disaster recovery involves the process of recovering data, applications, and IT infrastructure after a catastrophic event, such as a natural disaster, cyberattack, hardware failure, or human error. Cloud services offer several advantages for disaster recovery:

1. Scalability and Flexibility

Cloud services enable businesses to scale disaster recovery resources up or down as needed. This scalability ensures that companies can deploy recovery resources based on the size and complexity of their infrastructure, without the need for expensive on-premises hardware.

- **On-demand resources**: Cloud providers offer virtual machines, storage, and other resources that can be provisioned quickly in the event of a disaster, allowing organizations to restore operations without delay.

2. Geographic Redundancy

One of the most important advantages of cloud disaster recovery is geographic redundancy. Cloud providers maintain multiple data centers in different regions, allowing organizations to replicate their data and applications across different locations. This ensures that in the event of a local disaster (e.g., power outage, natural disaster), services can failover to a different region with minimal disruption.

- **AWS Availability Zones**: AWS provides multiple Availability Zones (AZs) within each region, each designed to be isolated from failures in other AZs.

- **Azure Availability Zones**: Similar to AWS, Azure provides multiple availability zones for geographic redundancy and fault isolation.

3. Cost-Effective Solutions

In traditional disaster recovery setups, businesses need to maintain dedicated hardware and infrastructure to handle potential disasters. This approach can be expensive. Cloud-based DR solutions allow organizations to use cloud resources only when needed, paying for them on a **pay-as-you-go** basis.

- **Cloud storage and compute**: Cloud services like **AWS S3**, **Azure Blob Storage**, and **Google Cloud Storage** allow organizations to store backup data cheaply and scale recovery resources based on demand.

4. Automation and Orchestration

Cloud-based disaster recovery solutions can automate much of the recovery process, from data replication to failover. Automation ensures faster recovery times and reduces human error during the recovery process.

- **Automated backups**: Cloud services like **AWS Backup** and **Azure Site Recovery** automate the process of backing up and recovering data.

- **Disaster recovery orchestration**: Cloud providers offer orchestration services that manage the entire recovery process, ensuring that all systems are restored in the correct order.

Setting Up Automated Backups and Failover Strategies

Setting up automated backups and failover strategies is essential for ensuring data protection and business continuity. Cloud providers offer a variety of tools and services to simplify this process.

1. Automated Backups

Automated backups are an essential component of disaster recovery. Cloud services provide flexible backup solutions that can be configured to back up data at regular intervals, ensuring that data is safe and can be restored quickly.

How to Set Up Automated Backups:

- **AWS Backup**: A fully managed backup service for AWS services like **EC2**, **RDS**, and **EFS**. AWS Backup allows you to create backup plans, automate backups, and monitor backup jobs.

- **Azure Backup**: A cloud-based backup service that protects data in virtual machines, applications, and file systems.
- **Google Cloud Backup and DR**: A managed service for protecting applications, databases, and virtual machines in Google Cloud.

Best Practices for Automated Backups:

- **Backup Frequency**: Set backup intervals that meet your Recovery Point Objective (RPO), i.e., how much data you can afford to lose. For critical data, backups should occur frequently, such as hourly or daily.
- **Backup Retention**: Define retention policies to ensure that older backups are deleted after a certain period, freeing up storage space and reducing costs.
- **Offsite Storage**: Ensure that backups are stored in geographically separate regions or availability zones for redundancy.

2. Failover Strategies

A failover strategy is the process of transferring operations from a failed system or region to a backup system or region. Cloud providers offer multiple failover solutions for achieving high availability and minimizing downtime.

Types of Failover Strategies:

- **Active-Active Failover**: Both primary and backup systems run simultaneously, and traffic is load-balanced between them. In the event of a failure, traffic is redirected to the backup system.

- **Active-Passive Failover**: The primary system is active, while the backup system is passive (inactive). When the primary system fails, the backup system takes over.

- **Cross-Region Failover**: Cloud services can replicate applications and data across different regions. If one region goes down, traffic is automatically redirected to another region.

How to Implement Failover:

- **Amazon Route 53**: AWS offers **Route 53** for DNS failover. By configuring health checks and routing policies, Route 53 can detect when a service is unavailable and automatically reroute traffic to a healthy instance in another region or availability zone.

- **Azure Traffic Manager**: Similar to AWS Route 53, Azure Traffic Manager allows you to define DNS-based routing policies for automatic failover and load balancing.

- **Google Cloud DNS**: Google Cloud offers DNS-based failover and load balancing, enabling quick recovery in the event of an outage.

3. Disaster Recovery Orchestration

Disaster recovery orchestration tools automate the entire recovery process, ensuring that applications and systems are restored in the correct sequence.

- **AWS Elastic Disaster Recovery (DRS)**: AWS DRS simplifies disaster recovery by automating the replication of on-premises systems to AWS. In the event of a failure, it can quickly bring the system online in the cloud.
- **Azure Site Recovery (ASR)**: Azure Site Recovery automates the replication of virtual machines to Azure, enabling seamless failover and failback to the cloud.

Example: Setting Up a Backup Solution in AWS Using Glacier

In this section, we will set up a simple backup solution in **AWS** using **Amazon S3 Glacier**, a low-cost cloud storage service designed for data archiving and long-term backups.

Step 1: Create an S3 Bucket for Backup Storage

1. **Log in to AWS**: Go to the AWS Management Console and navigate to the **S3** service.
2. **Create a New Bucket**:

- o Click **Create Bucket**.
- o Enter a unique name for your bucket (e.g., `my-backup-bucket`).
- o Choose a region where you want your backups to be stored.
- o Click **Create**.

Step 2: Set Up S3 Glacier Storage Class

1. **Enable Glacier Storage Class**:
   - o When uploading files to S3, you can choose the **S3 Glacier** storage class for long-term storage.
   - o Navigate to your S3 bucket, and click **Upload**.
   - o Select files you want to back up.
   - o Under the **Storage Class**, select **Glacier** to ensure your data is stored in Amazon Glacier.

Step 3: Set Up Lifecycle Policies for Automated Backups

1. **Create a Lifecycle Policy**:
   - o In the S3 dashboard, click on the **Management** tab of your bucket.
   - o Click **Create lifecycle rule**.
   - o Name the rule (e.g., `Move to Glacier`).
   - o Define when objects should transition to Glacier. For example, you can set it to transition objects to Glacier after 30 days.

o Set additional actions like **expire** or **delete** objects after a certain period.

2. **Apply the Lifecycle Rule**:

o Save and apply the lifecycle rule to your bucket, ensuring that data is automatically transitioned to Glacier after the defined period.

Step 4: Backup Automation with AWS Backup

1. **Use AWS Backup for Automated Backups**:

o Go to the **AWS Backup** service in the console.

o Click **Create backup plan**.

o Choose the **S3 bucket** as the source and configure the frequency for backups (e.g., daily, weekly).

o Set the **storage class** to Glacier for long-term archiving.

o Define retention policies for how long backups should be kept before they are deleted.

Step 5: Monitor Backups

1. **Check Backup Status**:

o Use **AWS Backup** or the **S3 console** to monitor the status of your backups.

o Ensure that backups are being transitioned to Glacier as per the lifecycle policy.

Conclusion

In this chapter, we discussed the importance of **disaster recovery (DR)** and **backup solutions** in the cloud and how cloud services can help businesses implement these strategies effectively. We explored different failover strategies, automated backup solutions, and disaster recovery orchestration.

We also provided an example of setting up a **backup solution in AWS using Glacier**, which demonstrated how to leverage cloud services for efficient, low-cost data backup and disaster recovery. By implementing cloud-based disaster recovery and backup solutions, organizations can ensure data protection, minimize downtime, and maintain business continuity, even in the event of a disaster.

CHAPTER 23

BUILDING SCALABLE APPS IN THE CLOUD

One of the key advantages of cloud computing is the ability to scale applications based on demand. Whether you're handling an unexpected traffic surge, seasonal spikes, or consistent growth, cloud environments allow you to scale your applications easily, ensuring performance and reliability. In this chapter, we'll explore how to design cloud applications that can scale with demand, discuss auto-scaling and load balancing concepts, and provide an example of using **AWS Auto Scaling** to handle traffic spikes.

Designing Cloud Applications that Scale with Demand

Scalability is a fundamental principle of cloud computing. Cloud-based applications must be designed to handle fluctuating traffic loads without compromising performance, availability, or user experience. Designing scalable applications involves understanding how to distribute workloads efficiently and managing resources that can scale automatically.

1. Stateless Architecture

To ensure scalability, cloud applications are typically designed as **stateless** systems. This means that each request is independent of the others, and no session information is stored locally on any server. Stateless architectures make it easy to add or remove servers as needed without worrying about losing session data.

- **Example**: An API endpoint that handles user requests can run on multiple instances without sharing session state. This allows the application to scale horizontally by adding more instances as traffic increases.

2. Microservices Architecture

Building applications using a **microservices architecture** allows each component of the application to scale independently based on demand. Microservices are smaller, loosely coupled units of functionality that communicate with each other through APIs. This approach provides flexibility because individual services can be scaled based on their workload, without impacting other services.

- **Example**: In an e-commerce application, the **inventory service** may require more resources during a sales event, while the **payment service** may need fewer resources. With microservices, each service can be scaled independently.

3. Cloud-Native Services

Cloud-native services are designed to scale automatically as demand increases. When building scalable applications in the cloud, leveraging cloud-native services such as **serverless computing**, **managed databases**, and **storage services** can significantly reduce the complexity of scaling.

- **Example**: **AWS Lambda** allows you to run code without provisioning servers, automatically scaling based on the number of requests. This makes it an ideal solution for applications with variable traffic.

4. Database Scalability

When designing cloud applications, it's essential to consider how your database will scale. Databases need to handle large volumes of data while maintaining high performance. There are two types of scalability to consider:

- **Vertical scaling (scale-up)**: Increasing the capacity of a single instance by adding more CPU, memory, or storage.
- **Horizontal scaling (scale-out)**: Adding more instances or nodes to distribute the database load.

Cloud services like **Amazon RDS** (for relational databases) and **Amazon DynamoDB** (for NoSQL databases) offer automatic scaling options to handle traffic spikes and large data volumes.

Auto-scaling and Load Balancing Concepts

1. Auto-scaling

Auto-scaling is a cloud service feature that automatically adjusts the number of compute instances in response to changes in demand. It ensures that applications have enough resources to handle traffic spikes without over-provisioning and incurring unnecessary costs during low traffic periods.

Key Concepts in Auto-scaling:

- **Scaling Policies**: Auto-scaling works based on predefined policies that define when to add or remove instances. These policies are often based on metrics like CPU utilization, memory usage, or incoming request counts.
- **Scaling Up vs. Scaling Out**:
  - **Scaling up (vertical scaling)** involves adding more resources (e.g., CPU or memory) to a single instance.
  - **Scaling out (horizontal scaling)** involves adding more instances to distribute the load.
- **Elasticity**: Cloud auto-scaling provides elasticity, allowing resources to automatically adjust based on demand. This ensures that you're not over-provisioning

during off-peak times or under-provisioning during traffic spikes.

2. Load Balancing

Load balancing distributes incoming traffic across multiple servers or instances, ensuring that no single server is overwhelmed with too much traffic. It improves performance and ensures high availability by rerouting traffic to healthy instances in case of failures.

Key Concepts in Load Balancing:

- **Layer 4 Load Balancing**: Operates at the transport layer, distributing traffic based on IP address and port.
- **Layer 7 Load Balancing**: Operates at the application layer, allowing routing decisions based on the content of the request, such as URL, HTTP headers, or cookies.
- **Health Checks**: Load balancers continuously monitor the health of instances and reroute traffic away from instances that are down or underperforming.

Cloud providers offer managed load balancing services that make it easy to set up and manage load balancing for your applications.

AWS Example: **Elastic Load Balancing (ELB)** is a fully managed load balancing service that automatically distributes incoming traffic across multiple EC2 instances, containers, or IP addresses. It supports both Layer 4 (TCP) and Layer 7 (HTTP/HTTPS) load balancing.

3. Combining Auto-scaling and Load Balancing

By combining **auto-scaling** with **load balancing**, cloud applications can automatically adjust to changing traffic patterns and maintain optimal performance. The auto-scaling group increases or decreases the number of instances based on demand, while the load balancer ensures that traffic is evenly distributed across the instances.

Example: Using AWS Auto Scaling to Handle Traffic Spikes

Let's walk through an example of using **AWS Auto Scaling** to handle traffic spikes for a web application running on **EC2 instances**.

Step 1: Set Up an EC2 Instance

1. **Launch an EC2 Instance**:
   o Go to the **AWS EC2 Console** and launch an EC2 instance using an appropriate Amazon Machine Image (AMI) and instance type.

o   Install your web application (e.g., a Node.js app or a WordPress site) on the EC2 instance.

Step 2: Create an Auto Scaling Group

1. **Create an Auto Scaling Group**:

   o   In the **EC2 Dashboard**, go to the **Auto Scaling Groups** section and click **Create Auto Scaling Group**.

   o   Choose the EC2 instance you launched as the base configuration.

   o   Set the desired capacity (e.g., 1 instance), minimum capacity (e.g., 1 instance), and maximum capacity (e.g., 5 instances).

2. **Configure Scaling Policies**:

   o   Set scaling policies to add or remove instances based on certain criteria, such as CPU utilization or request count.

   o   For example, you can set the policy to add more instances when CPU utilization exceeds 70% for a sustained period or to remove instances when CPU utilization drops below 30%.

3. **Set Up Health Checks**:

   o   AWS Auto Scaling will periodically check the health of the instances. If an instance fails the health check, it will be replaced automatically with a healthy instance.

Step 3: Set Up Load Balancing

1. **Create an Elastic Load Balancer (ELB)**:
   - Go to the **EC2 Dashboard** and create a new **Application Load Balancer (ALB)**.
   - Configure listeners for HTTP and HTTPS traffic, and define the security group to allow inbound traffic on port 80 (HTTP) or 443 (HTTPS).
   - Add the EC2 instances (or Auto Scaling group) to the load balancer's target group.

2. **Configure Health Checks for Load Balancer**:
   - Set up health checks for the load balancer to monitor the health of the EC2 instances. If an instance is deemed unhealthy, traffic will be rerouted to healthy instances automatically.

Step 4: Test Auto Scaling and Load Balancing

1. **Simulate Traffic Spikes**:
   - To simulate traffic spikes, you can use tools like **Apache JMeter** or **Loader.io** to generate high traffic to your application.

2. **Observe Auto Scaling**:
   - As the traffic increases and CPU utilization exceeds the threshold you set, AWS Auto Scaling will add more EC2 instances to handle the additional load.

3. **Monitor Load Balancer Behavior**:

   o Use the **Elastic Load Balancer** to monitor how it distributes incoming traffic across the available EC2 instances.

   o If any instance fails, the load balancer will reroute traffic to healthy instances without downtime.

Step 5: Monitor Performance

1. **CloudWatch Metrics**:

   o Use **Amazon CloudWatch** to monitor the performance of your EC2 instances, Auto Scaling groups, and load balancers.

   o Set up CloudWatch alarms to notify you when scaling policies are triggered or when the load balancer detects unhealthy instances.

Conclusion

In this chapter, we explored how to **build scalable applications in the cloud**, focusing on designing cloud applications that can scale with demand. We discussed the concepts of **auto-scaling** and **load balancing**, which are essential for handling fluctuations in traffic while maintaining optimal performance and availability. Additionally, we provided a hands-on example of using **AWS**

Auto Scaling and **Elastic Load Balancing** to handle traffic spikes and ensure that a web application remains responsive under varying loads.

By designing applications with scalability in mind and leveraging the power of cloud-native tools like auto-scaling and load balancing, businesses can build applications that provide a seamless user experience, even during high-traffic events.

CHAPTER 24

CLOUD COLLABORATION TOOLS

Cloud collaboration tools have revolutionized the way teams work together, regardless of their physical locations. By leveraging cloud technology, organizations can ensure seamless communication, document sharing, and project management, all while benefiting from real-time collaboration. In this chapter, we'll explore popular cloud-based collaboration and productivity tools such as **Google Workspace** and **Office 365**, discuss how these tools enhance team collaboration, and provide an example of setting up a **shared Google Drive** for team file sharing.

Using Cloud-based Collaboration and Productivity Tools

Cloud collaboration tools allow teams to work together efficiently without being limited by geographic location. These tools offer features like document editing, file sharing, video conferencing, and task management, all integrated into a cohesive platform.

1. Google Workspace (formerly G Suite)

Google Workspace is a cloud-based suite of productivity tools that includes everything a team needs to collaborate effectively. It includes applications like **Google Docs, Google Sheets, Google Slides, Gmail, Google Meet**, and **Google Drive**.

Key Features:

- **Real-time Document Collaboration**: Multiple users can edit the same document, spreadsheet, or presentation simultaneously, making it easy to work on projects together.
- **Cloud Storage**: Google Drive provides cloud storage for files, which can be accessed and shared across devices.
- **Communication Tools**: **Google Meet** offers video conferencing capabilities, and **Google Chat** enables team communication in channels or direct messages.
- **Seamless Integration**: All Google Workspace apps integrate seamlessly with each other, allowing for a unified work experience.

How it Improves Collaboration:

- **Real-time Collaboration**: Google Workspace allows teams to collaborate in real time on documents, meaning everyone can contribute simultaneously without the need for emailing file versions back and forth.
- **Accessibility**: Since all documents are stored in the cloud, team members can access files from anywhere, whether they're in the office, at home, or on the go.

- **Version Control**: Google Docs automatically saves versions of a document, making it easy to track changes and revert to previous versions if needed.

2. Microsoft Office 365 (now Microsoft 365)

Microsoft 365 is another popular suite of cloud-based productivity tools that includes well-known applications such as **Word**, **Excel**, **PowerPoint**, **Teams**, **Outlook**, and **OneDrive**.

Key Features:

- **Real-time Co-authoring**: Just like Google Workspace, Microsoft 365 allows users to collaborate on documents in real time, whether they are working in **Word**, **Excel**, or **PowerPoint**.
- **Cloud Storage with OneDrive**: **OneDrive** provides cloud storage for files, which can be accessed, edited, and shared from any device.
- **Teams for Communication**: **Microsoft Teams** offers chat, video conferencing, file sharing, and integration with other Microsoft apps, making it an all-in-one tool for team collaboration.
- **Email and Calendar with Outlook**: **Outlook** provides email and calendar tools, with cloud-based syncing across all devices.

How it Improves Collaboration:

261

- **Integrated Communication**: **Teams** allows real-time messaging, voice, and video calls, all in one place, which can reduce the need for multiple communication tools.
- **Document Collaboration**: Users can co-author documents, track changes, and comment on files, helping teams work together more efficiently on shared projects.
- **Centralized Workspace**: Microsoft 365 integrates with tools like **Planner** and **To-Do**, helping teams manage tasks, assign work, and track deadlines all within the same platform.

3. Slack

Slack is a cloud-based team collaboration tool primarily focused on communication. It enables teams to stay in touch through channels, direct messages, and file sharing.

Key Features:

- **Channels**: Teams can organize conversations by topic, project, or department through channels, ensuring that information is easy to find and follow.
- **File Sharing**: Slack allows users to upload and share files, images, and documents directly in conversations.
- **Searchable History**: All conversations and files are stored in a searchable archive, making it easy to find past discussions or shared resources.

How it Improves Collaboration:

- **Instant Communication**: Slack provides real-time messaging, which is more efficient than email for quick exchanges.

- **Integration with Other Tools**: Slack integrates with a wide range of third-party applications, such as Google Workspace, Microsoft 365, and project management tools like **Trello** and **Asana**, allowing teams to access all the tools they need in one place.

- **Custom Notifications**: Slack's customizable notification settings ensure that team members are only alerted to the most relevant updates.

4. Trello and Asana (for Project Management)

Trello and **Asana** are cloud-based project management tools that help teams plan, track, and manage their tasks and projects.

- **Trello**: Trello uses a **kanban board** to organize tasks into boards, lists, and cards, making it easy to visualize workflows and progress. It's simple, flexible, and ideal for smaller teams or less complex projects.

- **Asana**: Asana provides more advanced project management features, including task dependencies, timelines, and team collaboration tools. It's better suited for larger teams or complex projects.

Key Features:

- **Task Assignment**: Both Trello and Asana allow users to assign tasks, set deadlines, and track progress.
- **Collaboration**: Team members can comment on tasks, upload files, and provide status updates.
- **Visualization**: Asana offers Gantt charts and timeline views, while Trello provides boards and cards for more intuitive task tracking.

How it Improves Collaboration:

- **Clear Task Management**: Both tools provide clarity on who is responsible for which tasks, reducing confusion and improving accountability.
- **Transparency**: Teams can see the status of all tasks, which fosters better communication and coordination.
- **Automation**: Both tools offer automation features that reduce manual work, such as setting recurring tasks or automatic notifications when a task is completed.

How Cloud Collaboration Tools Improve Team Collaboration in the Cloud

Cloud collaboration tools make it easier for teams to work together, even when they are not in the same location. These tools improve collaboration in several ways:

1. Real-Time Communication and Collaboration

- Cloud-based tools like **Google Docs**, **Microsoft Teams**, and **Slack** allow team members to work together in real-time, reducing delays and improving the speed of decision-making. Changes are immediately visible to all members, eliminating the need to exchange file versions or wait for updates.

2. Accessibility

- Cloud collaboration tools ensure that team members can access documents and resources from anywhere, whether they are in the office, at home, or on the go. This accessibility promotes flexibility and enables remote or distributed teams to work together seamlessly.

3. Centralized Data and Resources

- Cloud services like **Google Drive**, **OneDrive**, and **Slack** ensure that all files, communications, and project details are stored in one central location. This eliminates silos and makes it easier to find information, collaborate on documents, and manage tasks.

4. Version Control and History

- Many cloud collaboration tools automatically save document versions, allowing teams to track changes, revert to previous versions, and understand the history of their work. This ensures that everyone is on the same page and can easily recover from mistakes.

5. Scalability

- Cloud collaboration tools are scalable, meaning they can support teams of all sizes, from small startups to large enterprises. Organizations can easily add new team members, integrate new tools, and expand their workflows without the need for additional infrastructure.

Example: Setting Up a Shared Google Drive for Team File Sharing

Let's walk through an example of how to set up a **shared Google Drive** for team file sharing in **Google Workspace**.

Step 1: Set Up Google Workspace

If your organization hasn't already set up Google Workspace, go to the **Google Workspace website** and sign up for an account.

Once you've created your account, you can access **Google Drive**, **Gmail**, **Google Docs**, and other Google tools.

Step 2: Create a Shared Drive

1. **Access Google Drive**: Go to **drive.google.com**.
2. **Create a Shared Drive**:
    -   On the left-hand side, click **Shared drives**.
    -   Click + **New** and select **Create a new shared drive**.
    -   Name the shared drive (e.g., "Team Files" or "Project Documents").

Step 3: Set Permissions for Team Members

1. **Add Members**:
    -   Click on the **Shared drive** you created.
    -   Click on the **Manage members** button in the top-right corner.
    -   Enter the email addresses of the team members you want to add.
2. **Assign Roles**:
    -   Choose the appropriate role for each member (e.g., **Manager, Content Manager, Contributor**, or **Viewer**).

  o Set roles based on the level of access and permissions you want each team member to have (e.g., the ability to edit, comment, or view files).

Step 4: Upload and Share Files

1. **Upload Files**: Drag and drop files from your computer into the **Shared drive** to upload them.
2. **Organize Files**: Create folders within the shared drive to organize files by project, department, or any other category relevant to your team.
3. **Share Files**: Files in the shared drive can be accessed by everyone with the appropriate permissions. Team members can edit, comment, or view files based on their assigned role.

Step 5: Collaborate on Files

- Team members can collaborate on Google Docs, Sheets, and Slides directly within the shared drive. Changes are automatically saved, and team members can see real-time updates.
- Comments and suggestions can be added, making it easy to review and provide feedback on documents.

Conclusion

In this chapter, we explored the importance of **cloud collaboration tools** and how they enable seamless communication, document sharing, and project management for teams. We reviewed popular tools like **Google Workspace**, **Microsoft 365**, **Slack**, and **Trello**, and discussed how they improve collaboration by providing real-time, cloud-based solutions for teams of all sizes.

We also walked through the steps of setting up a **shared Google Drive** for team file sharing, which can serve as a central hub for storing and collaborating on important documents. By leveraging cloud collaboration tools, organizations can streamline workflows, enhance communication, and improve productivity, regardless of team members' locations.

CHAPTER 25

CLOUD FOR DEVOPS

In modern software development, **DevOps** has become a standard practice that emphasizes collaboration between development and operations teams to improve the speed, quality, and reliability of software delivery. The cloud plays a critical role in enabling and enhancing DevOps practices by providing scalable, flexible, and automated tools for continuous integration (CI), continuous deployment (CD), infrastructure as code (IaC), and monitoring. In this chapter, we will discuss how cloud platforms integrate with DevOps practices, the benefits of using the cloud for CI/CD, and provide a hands-on example of setting up **Docker**, **Jenkins**, and **Kubernetes** for DevOps in the cloud.

How Cloud Platforms Integrate with DevOps Practices

Cloud platforms offer a wide range of services and tools that seamlessly integrate with **DevOps** practices. These tools automate many aspects of the software delivery pipeline, from writing code to deployment and monitoring. Cloud providers like **AWS**, **Azure**, and **Google Cloud** provide DevOps services that help automate, scale, and monitor every stage of the software lifecycle.

1. Cloud Infrastructure as Code (IaC)

Infrastructure as Code (IaC) is a key principle of DevOps, where infrastructure is managed and provisioned using code, allowing teams to define, provision, and manage infrastructure in a repeatable and automated manner. Cloud platforms support IaC by providing services such as:

- **AWS CloudFormation**: A service that allows you to define cloud infrastructure in JSON or YAML templates, which can be versioned and reused.
- **Azure Resource Manager (ARM)**: Provides a way to define and deploy cloud resources in Azure using JSON templates.
- **Google Cloud Deployment Manager**: Allows users to define their Google Cloud infrastructure using configuration files.

These tools allow DevOps teams to treat infrastructure just like application code — they can version it, automate it, and deploy it in a consistent and repeatable manner.

2. Continuous Integration and Continuous Deployment (CI/CD)

CI/CD pipelines are essential to DevOps practices. They enable teams to integrate new code frequently, automatically test it, and deploy it to production in an automated way. Cloud platforms offer powerful services that integrate with CI/CD tools, making it easier to manage the process.

- **AWS CodePipeline**: An automated CI/CD service for AWS that allows you to model, visualize, and automate the steps required to release software.
- **Azure DevOps**: Provides a comprehensive set of tools for building CI/CD pipelines, managing repositories, and collaborating on code.
- **Google Cloud Build**: A service that allows you to automate the building and testing of applications, integrating easily with Google Cloud Storage and other services.

These services integrate with popular DevOps tools like **Jenkins**, **GitLab**, **Docker**, and **Kubernetes** to automate the end-to-end development and deployment pipeline.

3. Containerization and Orchestration

Cloud platforms make it easy to manage containers, which are central to modern DevOps workflows. **Docker** containers allow applications to be packaged with all their dependencies, making them portable and easy to deploy across different environments. **Kubernetes** is a container orchestration platform that automates the deployment, scaling, and management of containerized applications.

Cloud platforms like **AWS, Azure**, and **Google Cloud** provide fully managed container services, such as **Amazon ECS, Azure Kubernetes Service (AKS)**, and **Google Kubernetes Engine (GKE)**, which help teams deploy and manage applications using Docker and Kubernetes.

Benefits of Using Cloud for Continuous Integration and Deployment

Using the cloud for continuous integration and continuous deployment (CI/CD) brings several benefits, including faster development cycles, reduced manual effort, improved quality, and greater scalability.

1. Scalability

Cloud environments are inherently scalable, meaning they can automatically adjust resources based on the needs of the application. In DevOps, this scalability is vital for handling varying workloads during development, testing, and production. For example, when running CI/CD pipelines, the cloud can automatically scale the compute resources based on the number of builds and tests that need to be executed.

2. Automation and Efficiency

Cloud platforms offer services that automate various stages of the DevOps pipeline, reducing the need for manual intervention. Automated testing, code reviews, and deployments reduce the risk of errors and speed up the development lifecycle. For example, **AWS CodeBuild** can automatically build and test your code every time a change is pushed to the repository, and **Jenkins** can automatically trigger deployment pipelines.

3. Faster Time to Market

By automating the deployment pipeline and integrating tools like **Docker** and **Kubernetes**, development teams can quickly push new features and bug fixes into production. The ability to deploy code frequently and in smaller increments allows organizations to respond more quickly to customer needs, improving agility and competitive advantage.

4. Improved Collaboration

Cloud platforms provide collaborative environments where development and operations teams can work together more effectively. Cloud tools like **Jenkins**, **GitLab**, and **Slack** allow team members to communicate more efficiently, share progress, and manage code changes in real-time. This reduces friction and fosters a culture of continuous improvement and collaboration.

5. Cost Efficiency

Cloud-based CI/CD tools are typically more cost-effective than managing on-premises infrastructure. Cloud providers offer flexible pricing models, so you only pay for the resources you use. This is especially beneficial for small teams or startups that need to scale their infrastructure without investing in costly physical servers.

Example: Setting Up Docker, Jenkins, and Kubernetes for DevOps in the Cloud

Let's walk through an example of setting up **Docker, Jenkins**, and **Kubernetes** for a DevOps pipeline in the cloud. In this scenario, we will use **AWS** to manage the infrastructure, **Jenkins** for automation, **Docker** for containerization, and **Kubernetes** for orchestration.

Step 1: Set Up Docker

1. **Install Docker** on your local machine or CI/CD server.

   bash

   ```
   sudo apt-get install docker.io
   ```

2. **Create a Dockerfile**:

   o A Dockerfile defines the environment for your application. Here's a simple Dockerfile for a Node.js app:

```
Dockerfile

FROM node:14
WORKDIR /app
 package.json .
RUN npm install
 . .
CMD ["node", "app.js"]
```

3. **Build the Docker Image**:

   o Build the Docker image locally:

```bash
```

```
docker build -t my-node-app .
```

4. **Push the Docker Image to a Container Registry**:

   o You can push the image to a cloud container registry like **AWS ECR** or **Docker Hub**:

```bash
```

276

```
docker          tag          my-node-app:latest
<aws_account_id>.dkr.ecr.<region>.amazona
ws.com/my-node-app:latest
docker                                    push
<aws_account_id>.dkr.ecr.<region>.amazona
ws.com/my-node-app:latest
```

Step 2: Set Up Jenkins for CI/CD

1. **Install Jenkins** on an EC2 instance or use a pre-built Jenkins AMI from the AWS Marketplace.

2. **Configure Jenkins**:
   - o Once Jenkins is installed, configure the necessary plugins for Docker and Kubernetes.
   - o Create a new **Pipeline Job** in Jenkins that will automate the build and deployment process.

3. **Create a Jenkins Pipeline**:
   - o Define a Jenkinsfile for your CI/CD pipeline. Here's an example of a simple Jenkinsfile that builds a Docker image and deploys it to Kubernetes:

```groovy
pipeline {
    agent any
    stages {
        stage('Build Docker Image') {
            steps {
```

```
                    script {
                        sh 'docker build -t
my-node-app .'
                        sh 'docker tag my-
node-app:latest
<aws_account_id>.dkr.ecr.<region>.amazona
ws.com/my-node-app:latest'
                        sh 'docker push
<aws_account_id>.dkr.ecr.<region>.amazona
ws.com/my-node-app:latest'
                    }
                }
            }
            stage('Deploy to Kubernetes') {
                steps {
                    script {
                        sh 'kubectl apply -f
k8s/deployment.yaml'
                    }
                }
            }
        }
    }
```

Step 3: Set Up Kubernetes on AWS (EKS)

1. **Create an EKS Cluster**:
   o   Use **AWS EKS** to create a Kubernetes cluster.
       You can do this via the **AWS Management
       Console** or the **AWS CLI**.

278

```
bash
```

```
aws eks create-cluster --name my-cluster -
-role-arn  <role-arn>   --resources-vpc-
config              subnetIds=<subnet-
ids>,securityGroupIds=<security-group-
ids>
```

2. **Configure kubectl** to interact with your EKS Cluster:

```
bash
```

```
aws  eks  update-kubeconfig  --name  my-
cluster
```

3. **Create Kubernetes Deployment and Service Files**:
   o Define your Kubernetes deployment in a YAML
   file (e.g., `deployment.yaml`):

```
yaml
```

```yaml
apiVersion: apps/v1
kind: Deployment
metadata:
  name: my-node-app
spec:
  replicas: 3
  selector:
    matchLabels:
      app: my-node-app
```

279

```
template:
  metadata:
    labels:
      app: my-node-app
  spec:
    containers:
    - name: my-node-app
      image:
<aws_account_id>.dkr.ecr.<region>.amazona
ws.com/my-node-app:latest
      ports:
      - containerPort: 80
```

4. **Deploy the Application**:

   o Apply the deployment and service configuration to Kubernetes:

```bash
```

```
kubectl apply -f deployment.yaml
```

Step 4: Automate the Pipeline

1. **Trigger the Jenkins Pipeline**:

   o Once Jenkins is set up with the Docker, Kubernetes, and AWS configurations, trigger the pipeline every time there is a change in your source code repository (e.g., GitHub).

o Jenkins will automatically build the Docker image, push it to ECR, and deploy the updated image to your Kubernetes cluster.

Conclusion

In this chapter, we explored how **cloud platforms** integrate with **DevOps practices** to facilitate automation, scalability, and faster delivery of software. We also discussed the benefits of using cloud services for **continuous integration (CI)** and **continuous deployment (CD)**, such as faster deployment times, improved collaboration, and increased reliability.

The example of setting up **Docker, Jenkins,** and **Kubernetes** in the cloud demonstrated how these tools work together to automate the process of building, testing, and deploying applications in a cloud environment. By leveraging cloud-based DevOps tools, organizations can improve the efficiency and scalability of their software development lifecycle, ensuring faster and more reliable application delivery.

CHAPTER 26

FUTURE OF CLOUD COMPUTING

Cloud computing has transformed the way businesses and individuals access and utilize computing resources. As the demand for faster, more efficient, and scalable services continues to grow, the future of cloud computing is being shaped by emerging technologies such as **edge computing**, **quantum computing**, and **multi-cloud strategies**. These trends promise to further disrupt industries and enhance cloud capabilities. In this chapter, we will explore these trends, discuss how emerging technologies will shape the future of cloud computing, and provide an example of how **edge computing** works alongside cloud services.

Trends in Cloud Computing: Edge Computing, Quantum Computing, and Multi-cloud Strategies

1. Edge Computing

What is Edge Computing?
Edge computing refers to the practice of processing data closer to its source, at the "edge" of the network, rather than relying solely on centralized cloud data centers. In edge computing, data is processed locally on devices or edge servers, reducing latency,

bandwidth usage, and dependency on cloud data centers for real-time data processing.

Why Edge Computing is Important:

- **Reduced Latency**: By processing data closer to the source, edge computing significantly reduces the time it takes for data to travel to a centralized cloud server and back, which is crucial for applications requiring real-time responses (e.g., autonomous vehicles, IoT devices).
- **Lower Bandwidth Usage**: Edge computing reduces the amount of data that needs to be sent to the cloud for processing, which helps save bandwidth and reduce operational costs.
- **Reliability**: Edge computing can continue to function even when the connection to the cloud is lost, as local processing can handle tasks independently.

Applications of Edge Computing:

- **IoT (Internet of Things)**: Edge computing is particularly relevant for IoT devices that generate large volumes of data, such as smart sensors, wearables, and industrial machines.
- **Autonomous Vehicles**: Vehicles that rely on real-time data from cameras, sensors, and other devices can benefit

from edge computing, allowing them to make quick decisions without waiting for cloud processing.

- **Smart Cities**: Edge computing enables smart infrastructure such as traffic management systems, surveillance cameras, and environmental monitoring systems to process data locally and respond quickly to changes.

2. Quantum Computing

What is Quantum Computing? Quantum computing is an emerging technology that uses quantum mechanics to process information in ways that traditional computers cannot. Unlike classical computers that use bits to represent data (either 0 or 1), quantum computers use **qubits**, which can represent multiple states simultaneously due to quantum superposition.

Why Quantum Computing is Important:

- **Unprecedented Computing Power**: Quantum computing has the potential to solve problems that are currently unsolvable by classical computers, especially in fields like cryptography, material science, and complex simulations.
- **Speed**: Quantum computers could exponentially accelerate tasks such as optimizing logistics, drug

284

discovery, and climate modeling, making them valuable for industries that rely on massive data sets and intricate calculations.

- **Impact on Cloud Computing**: As quantum computers evolve, cloud providers may offer quantum computing as a service (QCaaS), enabling developers to run quantum algorithms without needing to own and maintain quantum hardware.

Applications of Quantum Computing:

- **Cryptography**: Quantum computing has the potential to break current encryption methods, prompting the need for new quantum-resistant encryption algorithms.
- **Pharmaceutical Research**: Quantum computing can simulate molecular structures, which can speed up drug discovery and help develop personalized medicines.
- **Optimization Problems**: Industries like logistics, transportation, and finance could benefit from quantum computing's ability to solve complex optimization problems faster and more accurately than classical computers.

3. Multi-cloud Strategies

What is a Multi-cloud Strategy?
A **multi-cloud strategy** involves using multiple cloud providers

(e.g., AWS, Azure, Google Cloud) for different parts of an organization's infrastructure. This approach allows businesses to avoid vendor lock-in, improve performance, and ensure redundancy and disaster recovery by distributing workloads across different cloud platforms.

Why Multi-cloud is Important:

- **Avoid Vendor Lock-In**: By using multiple cloud providers, businesses avoid becoming too dependent on one vendor, allowing them to switch providers if necessary without significant disruptions.
- **Optimized Performance**: Different cloud providers offer different strengths, and a multi-cloud approach allows businesses to choose the best provider for each specific use case.
- **Redundancy and Disaster Recovery**: A multi-cloud strategy provides backup and failover options by distributing workloads across different providers and regions, ensuring that services can continue even if one provider experiences an outage.

Applications of Multi-cloud:

- **Global Applications**: Organizations with a global user base can use multiple cloud providers to ensure high availability and low-latency access for users in different regions.

- **Disaster Recovery**: Multi-cloud setups can be used for disaster recovery purposes, with backups and failover mechanisms in place across different cloud platforms.

- **Optimizing Costs**: By choosing the most cost-effective cloud provider for each part of the infrastructure, businesses can reduce overall cloud expenses while still meeting performance and security requirements.

How Emerging Technologies Will Shape the Future of Cloud Computing

Emerging technologies like edge computing, quantum computing, and multi-cloud strategies are set to fundamentally reshape the future of cloud computing. Let's explore how these technologies will impact cloud-based services.

1. Integration of Edge and Cloud Computing

Edge computing is not a replacement for cloud computing but rather a complementary technology. As IoT devices and applications generate vast amounts of data, it becomes impractical to send all this data to the cloud for processing due to latency and bandwidth concerns. Instead, edge computing allows for local processing, and the cloud can be used for more intensive computational tasks, analytics, and long-term data storage.

- **Example**: In a smart city scenario, traffic cameras can process data locally (on the edge) to detect accidents or traffic congestion in real-time, but the historical data and analytics can be stored and processed in the cloud.
- **Cloud and Edge Synergy**: Cloud services will manage and analyze the large datasets that edge devices produce. For example, AWS **Greengrass** and Azure **IoT Edge** extend cloud computing capabilities to edge devices, enabling seamless integration and management.

2. Quantum Cloud Computing

Quantum computing will likely become a cloud service in the coming years, with cloud providers offering quantum computing as a service (QCaaS). This will make quantum computing accessible to businesses and researchers without requiring them to own or maintain quantum hardware.

- **Example**: Companies like **IBM** and **Google** are already offering quantum computing services through cloud platforms. As quantum computing becomes more mainstream, businesses will be able to access quantum processors through cloud APIs, using them for complex simulations or cryptographic tasks that are not possible with classical computers.

3. Multi-cloud as the New Norm

In the future, multi-cloud strategies will become more prevalent as organizations seek flexibility, resilience, and cost optimization. Cloud providers will focus on offering services that make it easier for organizations to manage workloads across multiple clouds, with improved interoperability, migration tools, and hybrid solutions.

- **Example**: A large enterprise might use **Google Cloud** for big data analytics, **AWS** for storage, and **Microsoft Azure** for machine learning, allowing each cloud provider to offer the best solution for different use cases while minimizing risk and improving resilience.

Example: How Edge Computing Works Alongside Cloud Services

Let's walk through an example of how **edge computing** works in conjunction with cloud services in a smart manufacturing scenario.

289

Step 1: Edge Devices Collect Data

In a smart factory, IoT devices such as **sensors**, **cameras**, and **machines** collect data about the manufacturing process, including machine temperature, speed, and product quality. This data is crucial for maintaining equipment and ensuring production quality, but transmitting all this data to the cloud in real-time would create significant latency and bandwidth issues.

Step 2: Local Processing on Edge Devices

Using **edge computing**, the data is processed locally at the edge (on the factory floor) by **edge devices** or **edge servers**. These devices can analyze data such as temperature readings or machine performance in real time to detect anomalies and predict maintenance needs. For example:

- If a sensor detects that a machine is overheating, the edge device can immediately trigger an alarm or take action to shut down the machine to prevent damage.

Step 3: Cloud Integration for Long-Term Analytics

While edge devices handle real-time decision-making, the cloud is used for long-term storage, in-depth analysis, and reporting. Data from the edge devices can be periodically sent to the cloud for further analysis, such as aggregating data from multiple factories, conducting predictive maintenance analysis, or generating business intelligence reports.

- **Example**: The cloud platform, such as **AWS IoT Core** or **Azure IoT Hub**, collects and stores data from the edge devices, allowing managers to analyze trends over time, identify patterns, and optimize production processes across the entire network of factories.

Step 4: Decision-Making Across Both Edge and Cloud

In this hybrid architecture, edge devices are responsible for making real-time decisions and actions, while the cloud provides centralized management, data aggregation, and advanced analytics. Both work together to optimize performance, reduce latency, and enhance efficiency.

Conclusion

The future of cloud computing is shaped by emerging technologies like **edge computing**, **quantum computing**, and **multi-cloud strategies**. These trends will enable faster processing, greater flexibility, and more efficient use of resources across industries. Edge computing complements cloud services by handling real-time data processing at the edge of the network, reducing latency, and improving performance. Meanwhile,

quantum computing will bring new computational capabilities to the cloud, and **multi-cloud strategies** will provide businesses with the flexibility to optimize their infrastructure across different providers.

By embracing these emerging technologies, cloud computing will continue to evolve, enabling more powerful, efficient, and scalable solutions that can meet the ever-growing demands of businesses and consumers.

CHAPTER 27

CLOUD APPLICATION CASE STUDIES

Cloud computing has transformed the way businesses and organizations build, deploy, and manage applications. Successful cloud implementations can drive innovation, enhance operational efficiency, and improve scalability. However, not every cloud migration or application design is flawless, and understanding both successful case studies and failures provides valuable lessons for future projects. In this chapter, we will explore real-world case studies of successful cloud implementations, the lessons learned from cloud application failures, and discuss **Netflix's use of AWS** as a notable example.

Real-World Case Studies of Successful Cloud Implementations

1. Netflix on AWS

Overview:

Netflix, the global leader in video streaming, migrated to the cloud to improve scalability, reliability, and global availability. Netflix transitioned from traditional on-premises data centers to Amazon

Web Services (AWS), relying on cloud services to handle massive amounts of data and user traffic across the world.

Why Netflix Moved to the Cloud:

- **Scalability**: Netflix's on-premise data centers couldn't handle the exponential growth in demand for streaming content, especially during peak usage times.
- **Global Reach**: To provide high-quality streaming to its global audience, Netflix needed a solution that would enable it to deliver content at scale and maintain a smooth user experience in different regions.
- **Resilience**: The ability to deliver uninterrupted service, even in the event of failures, was critical to Netflix's reputation and business model.

Cloud Services Used:

- **Amazon EC2**: Netflix utilizes Amazon EC2 instances for running compute resources to scale up or down based on traffic.
- **Amazon S3**: Netflix stores its vast content library (movies, TV shows, etc.) on Amazon S3 for highly available, scalable storage.
- **Amazon CloudFront**: CloudFront, AWS's content delivery network (CDN), delivers content to users quickly

by caching copies of videos at edge locations closer to the user.

- **AWS Lambda**: Netflix uses serverless computing with AWS Lambda to automate tasks like encoding, rendering, and processing large video files.

Key Outcomes:

- **Scalable and Reliable Streaming**: The cloud infrastructure allows Netflix to scale dynamically based on demand, especially during peak times or content launches.
- **Global Expansion**: By using AWS, Netflix can provide streaming services to viewers in over 190 countries, delivering content with low latency and high performance.
- **Resilience and Failover**: Netflix uses a **multi-AZ (Availability Zone)** setup, which ensures that even if one data center experiences a failure, another data center can seamlessly take over.

Lessons Learned:

- **Cloud Is Essential for Global Scalability**: The move to AWS allowed Netflix to scale rapidly and deliver consistent performance to users worldwide.

- **Embrace Resilience and Redundancy**: Building resilient, multi-availability-zone architectures ensures that services remain available even during unexpected failures.
- **Automate for Efficiency**: Netflix's use of AWS Lambda and automation tools enables it to handle large-scale data processing tasks efficiently without manual intervention.

2. Airbnb on AWS

Overview:

Airbnb, a popular online marketplace for lodging and travel experiences, also transitioned its infrastructure to AWS to handle scaling challenges and to improve reliability for its growing user base.

Why Airbnb Moved to the Cloud:

- **Scalability**: As Airbnb's user base grew, its on-premise infrastructure became difficult to scale quickly to accommodate new features and increased traffic.
- **Cost Efficiency**: With AWS, Airbnb could avoid the upfront cost of building physical data centers and instead use a pay-as-you-go model based on demand.
- **Flexibility**: Airbnb needed an environment that allowed developers to iterate quickly, experiment with new features, and deploy them on a global scale.

Cloud Services Used:

- **Amazon EC2**: Airbnb uses EC2 instances to host its website and backend services, scaling up or down based on demand.
- **Amazon S3**: S3 is used for storing large amounts of data such as images and files uploaded by users.
- **AWS RDS**: For Airbnb's relational database needs, AWS RDS (Relational Database Service) ensures high availability, fault tolerance, and scalability for its PostgreSQL databases.

Key Outcomes:

- **Rapid Growth and Flexibility**: Airbnb can rapidly scale its infrastructure to accommodate user demand, including during peak times like holidays or special events.
- **Operational Efficiency**: With AWS, Airbnb shifted away from managing infrastructure to focusing more on delivering new features and improving user experience.
- **Improved Reliability**: Using AWS ensures that Airbnb has high availability, reducing the risk of downtime during high-demand periods.

Lessons Learned:

- **Cloud Enables Business Agility**: The move to AWS allowed Airbnb to respond quickly to business needs, such as increasing traffic during peak seasons.

- **Data Management and Scalability**: Cloud services like RDS and S3 offer scalable storage and database solutions that can grow with the business.

- **Avoid Over-Provisioning**: By using cloud infrastructure, Airbnb only pays for the resources it uses, avoiding unnecessary costs associated with over-provisioning on-premises infrastructure.

What Can Be Learned from Cloud Application Failures and Successes?

While there have been many successful cloud implementations, failures also offer valuable lessons. Understanding these lessons can help businesses avoid common pitfalls and ensure more successful cloud deployments.

1. Cloud Failures: Lessons from the Past

Case Study: The 2017 AWS S3 Outage

- **Incident**: In February 2017, an AWS S3 outage in the US-East-1 region caused significant downtime for a large number of websites and applications. This outage was caused by human error during routine maintenance, and it took several hours to resolve.

Key Lessons:

- **Implement Redundancy and Multi-Region Support**: The outage affected many services that relied on the US-East-1 region. Organizations should consider replicating critical data across multiple regions or availability zones to ensure high availability.
- **Monitor and Alerting**: AWS offers robust monitoring tools (like **CloudWatch**), but organizations must implement their own monitoring and alerting systems to catch potential issues before they lead to major failures.
- **Preparation for Failures**: Cloud providers are not immune to outages, so businesses must have disaster recovery plans in place, including automated failover mechanisms, to ensure business continuity.

2. Cloud Successes: Lessons Learned

Case Study: Dropbox's Migration to AWS

- **Overview**: Dropbox, the cloud file storage provider, migrated from its own data centers to AWS to improve scalability and efficiency. The company was able to offload infrastructure management to AWS, allowing its engineers to focus on building features rather than maintaining hardware.

Key Lessons:

- **Migrate in Phases**: Dropbox's successful migration was the result of careful planning, starting with smaller, less critical workloads and gradually moving to more complex services. This phased approach minimized risk.
- **Leverage Cloud-Native Services**: Dropbox utilized **AWS S3** for storage, **Amazon EC2** for computing, and other AWS services that optimized performance and provided scalability without requiring large upfront investments in hardware.

Example: How Edge Computing Works Alongside Cloud Services

Scenario: Smart Healthcare Devices in a Hospital

In a smart healthcare system, edge computing and cloud computing work together to deliver real-time, efficient services. For instance, consider a hospital using **IoT devices** to monitor patients' vitals, such as heart rate, blood pressure, and temperature.

Step 1: Data Collection at the Edge

- **Edge Devices** (e.g., IoT sensors) collect data about the patients' health metrics in real-time. These devices process the data locally to detect immediate concerns, such as abnormal heart rates or other health emergencies, and trigger alerts for medical staff.

Step 2: Local Data Processing

- The devices or local edge servers process the data locally to provide immediate feedback and alerts. This **low-latency processing** ensures that any critical events are handled quickly, without waiting for cloud communication.

Step 3: Cloud Integration for Long-Term Analysis

- Data from the edge devices is periodically uploaded to a **cloud platform** (e.g., AWS or Azure) for long-term storage and deeper analysis. The cloud handles more intensive tasks, such as:
  - **Aggregating patient data**: Combining patient data from multiple sources to provide a comprehensive health profile.
  - **Analytics**: Running machine learning models to predict patient risks or outcomes, such as early detection of diseases or potential complications.

- o **Archiving**: Storing the data securely and complying with healthcare regulations (e.g., HIPAA).

Step 4: Real-Time Decision-Making

- The cloud platform can also store historical data for future reference, allowing doctors to make more informed decisions based on trends, patterns, and historical patient health data.

In this hybrid model, **edge computing** ensures that patient data is processed in real-time and is immediately actionable, while **cloud services** provide scalable storage, long-term analytics, and the ability to integrate insights from different sources.

Conclusion

In this chapter, we explored real-world case studies of successful cloud implementations, such as **Netflix** and **Airbnb**, and examined what can be learned from both cloud successes and failures. These case studies reveal the importance of **scalability**, **resilience**, and **automation** in the cloud. We also delved into how **emerging technologies like edge computing** will work alongside cloud services to further enhance the capabilities of cloud applications, as demonstrated in the smart healthcare example.

The cloud continues to evolve, and as businesses and technologies grow, the future of cloud computing will be shaped by continued innovation and integration with other cutting-edge technologies. Whether you're migrating to the cloud or building new cloud applications, these lessons from past successes and failures can provide invaluable guidance.

www.ingramcontent.com/pod-product-compliance
Lightning Source LLC
LaVergne TN
LVHW022336060326
832902LV00022B/4061